Keeping Christmas

To/
Oscar, Dewena, & family

Merry Christmas 2015

Mom

Keeping Christmas

STORIES FROM THE HEART

DESERET BOOK COMPANY
SALT LAKE CITY, UTAH

Library of Congress Cataloging-in-Publication Data

Keeping Christmas : stories from the heart : compilation of various authors.
   p.   cm.
  ISBN 1-57345-198-3 (hc)
  1. Christmas—Miscellanea. 2. Church of Jesus Christ of Latter-day Saints—Miscellanea. 3. Mormon Church—Miscellanea.
BV45.S577   1996
263'.91—dc20   96-24326
                                                         CIP

Printed in the United States of America

10 9   8   7   6   5   4   3   2   1

Contents

"It Is Better to Give Than to Receive"

GEORGE D. DURRANT

CHRISTMAS WAS COMING, and each of us first graders in Miss Booth's class had drawn the name of another boy or girl to whom we were to give a Christmas gift. It was to cost no more than fifty cents.

On the day when the gifts were to be brought to school, I arrived early and put my gift for Walt under the Christmas tree. Then I sat in my seat waiting to see who would put a gift for me under the tree.

Bob came in with a big box wrapped in red paper with a large white ribbon. Each of the children hoped that this gift, which was by far the largest one, would be for him. Then Bob shouted, "This big present is for George."

I had never been so happy. The biggest present under the tree was for me! All the other children in the class wished that they were as lucky as I was. I could hardly wait for the end of the day, when the gifts would be opened. Many times that day a boy or girl would say to me, "You are so lucky. I wish I was you. I wish that the big present was for me."

Finally the time came. Miss Booth said, "All right, boys and girls, it is time to open the gifts. We are all so excited to see what is in that large present Bob got for George. So let's start with that one. Bob, would you come up and take your gift to lucky George?"

My heart pounded with excitement. All eyes were upon me. I could tell that everyone else wished they were me.

My heart pounded with excitement. I could tell that everyone else wished they were me.

Bob placed the large red box in front of me. I began to tear the paper away. Then I opened the box. I could see much crumpled-up newspaper. I pulled each of the papers from the box. Then, down at the bottom of the box, I saw a book. I pulled it out and saw it was a coloring book.

Suddenly all of my happiness changed to sadness. I didn't like coloring books.

Then everyone said, "I hope I don't get a coloring book. I hope I get something more exciting than what George got."

Now, instead of feeling like I was the happiest person in the world, I felt that I was the saddest. I didn't even want to watch to see what the other boys and girls received for their gifts. I even felt that I didn't like Bob, because Bob had made me feel unhappy.

Finally the teacher said, "Now for our last gift. It

is the gift that George brought for Walt. George, please come up and get your gift and give it to Walt."

As I walked to the front I felt sad. Everyone in the class had received a better gift than I had received. I took the gift to Walt and then I sat down.

A minute later Walt shouted, "Oh, look at this! This is what I wanted! It is a walkometer. You pin it on your belt and it will tell you how far you have walked."

Walt put it on his belt and began to walk around the room. All of the other boys and girls were really excited. One boy said, "I wish I had that. That is the best gift of all the gifts. I wish George had drawn my name."

A girl said, "Next year I hope that George gets my name."

Then Miss Booth said, "George, you sure do know how to give good gifts. Everyone in the class wants to be able to make others as happy as you have made Walt."

Walt turned around and looked at me and said, "Thanks, George, for making me the happiest boy in the class."

Suddenly I didn't feel sad inside. I looked at my coloring book and saw a picture of some pirates. I loved pirates. I wanted to get out my crayons and go to work, but it was time to go home.

As I left to go home Bob shouted, "Merry Christmas, George." I said the same thing back, and I felt that this would be my happiest Christmas so far.

GEORGE D. DURRANT *is the author of many books and cassette tapes, including* Love at Home—Starring Father; Someone Special—Starring YOUth; The Art of Raising Parents; Get Ready! Get Called! Go!; Fun and Names, or How to Dig Your Family History without Really Prying; Don't Forget the Star; Mother, Our Heavenly Connection; *and* Tom Trails: A New Beginning *(coauthored with Wayne B. Lynn). With his son Matthew he has coauthored two novels:* There's an Enemy Sub in Potter's Pond *and* Keeping Score. *A popular speaker, he is currently an institute teacher in the Church Educational System.*

A Season of Love and Service in Ireland

STEPHEN R. COVEY

FOR A MOMENT, I felt like I had slipped into the transcendent magic of a long-remembered fairy tale. The December cold of Belfast, the kind that shrouds the streets and pierces to the very core of heart and hearth, was wondrously replaced by a surging warmth I will never forget. I stood back in the crowd, allowing myself the supreme satisfaction of observing one of the rarest moments any mission president could ever experience. There they were, our missionaries, being followed like so many Pied Pipers by adoring children through the streets. Little Irish lads and lassies—their faces grimed with soot or chafed and red with cold, swathed in mended wool scarves and layers of patched sweaters—joyously teased toys and treats from young Mormon missionaries playing Father Christmas. I saw our Savior's light in the missionaries' faces as they greeted weeping, grateful parents, amazed storekeepers, and surprised shoppers, going from shop to shop and house to house, offering themselves in pure love and service.

Such is my treasured memory of Christmas 1962, my first year as president of the Irish Mission. It all started when teaching opportunities were eclipsed by Christmas busyness and made us take another look at what we were about. People were full of the Christmas season with its shopping, festivities, visiting, and various traditional celebrations. They were so busy celebrating Christ's birth that they didn't make time to learn of his mission. It was, therefore, the time when missionaries most easily lost focus in homesickness and longing for their own holiday traditions. So, on about the tenth of December, we decided that we should shift our entire strategy from one of finding and teaching to one of serving and friendshipping.

We had all the missionaries literally stop their traditional proselytizing activities and spend their time meeting human needs in every way they possibly could. I know the highest thing you can bring people is the gospel of Jesus Christ, but sometimes you have to prepare them for that, and it was the example of the Savior himself that guided us in our decision. Christ often served without agenda. He blessed only for the sake of blessing. He loved because it was needed. Later, he taught and the people flocked to him because they knew him. They responded to his ministry because they had felt of his ministrations.

So for the holiday weeks of December, our only

I was most forcibly struck with how cold their home was. You could see your breath in the air; you could see dampness frosting the wood furniture. As soon as I entered, the father hastened to turn on a little electric heater.

mission was to meet people, make friends, enter homes and assess needs, then go about with our greatest efforts to emulate Christlike love to meet those needs.

I remember knocking on the door of one particularly humble home, strangers, nonmembers. There was a mom and dad and many small children. I was most forcibly struck with how cold their home was. You could see your breath in the air; you could see dampness frosting the wood furniture. As soon as I entered, the father hastened to turn on a little electric heater in the front room. I later learned that there were small heaters in the two bedrooms, which they would turn on briefly before the children went to bed, then turn down again once they were asleep. There was so little money for heat they had no other choice.

My purpose (as was the purpose of all such visits that month in the mission) was to view this situation through Christ's eyes and then bless this family as I thought he might. I later returned with my wife, Sandra, and our three smallest children, Cynthia, age six, Maria, three, and Stephen M. R., still a baby. We brought with us blankets, food, clothes, and some money so the family could increase their heat. We also brought Christmas presents, which, of course, the children enjoyed most. I'll never forget the mixture of delight and wonder in those people's faces. I could see they were waiting for the catch. What was it we expected from them in return?

They soon enough had their answer. We

expected nothing. For those two or three weeks that December, our motive was service. Not service with the intent to teach. Just service.

The missionaries were beautiful. All across Ireland, young men and women—whom everyone knew were Mormons—met human needs in every way they possibly could. They combed the streets shaking hands. They went into people's homes asking, How can we serve you? How can we help? They helped decorate or made small repairs. They gave food to the poor, played with children, fetched and carried and ran errands, chopped wood, scrubbed floors, tended the sick—whatever came to mind and heart.

Even I couldn't resist the fun of dressing up as Father Christmas and visiting the homes of our members. Most of them didn't even know who I was, other than a jolly, boisterous person in a red suit who hugged the little kids and brought presents and candy. It was unbelievably satisfying and joyous to be totally in the service mode, with no other aim in mind.

Of course, we were rewarded beyond imagination. The missionaries wrote home telling their families of their grand experiences. They described the overwhelming sense of happiness and joy they experienced in going forth, as our Savior did, ministering to people. Letters back from parents to the mission home said they'd never seen their sons or daughters have such a glorious Christmas.

Floods of teaching opportunities met us downstream; three, four, even five times as many discussions were taught in the months of January through March as in previous months. It naturally followed, then, that we learned a great lesson about the value of renewal and the power of Christlike love. This season of service became our mission holiday tradition for the following two years while I was president.

One of the most tremendous benefits was that the missionaries got very close to the people. They loved the Irish people. Our group of missionaries later established the Shamrock Society, a nonprofit organization that continues to function today. They have, during the past thirty-plus years, contributed money to send out more than seventy Irish missionaries into the mission field, on the condition that they would return and build up their own country. I also believe that the spirit of the Shamrock Society keeps our missionaries united. We still draw more than 150 people annually to our reunions. We read touching, newsy letters full of support and gratitude from our "adopted children" serving in Ireland and can't help but feel the wonderful connection.

Personally, two important lessons were reinforced by this experience. First, joy comes in service. It's plain and simple, but true—and as mission president, I realized a double dose of joy in seeing the joy that came to our missionaries in creating happiness for others. Second, there's a season for everything. Half of the Savior's ministry was spent teaching, half in just

They combed the streets shaking hands. They went into people's homes asking, How can we serve you? They gave food to the poor, played with children, scrubbed floors, tended the sick—whatever came to mind and heart.

meeting people's needs. So it is with our teaching. We have to read the culture, whether it be as a missionary in a foreign country, a teacher in Primary, or a parent at home. There is a time to teach and a time to live the work of the Savior, which creates the ripe moments for teaching.

Those three Christmases in Ireland are my most memorable, not only because of the joy that Sandra and I had, but also because of the joy that we saw in the lives of our missionaries when they really learned to live outside themselves in love.

STEPHEN R. COVEY *is the founder and chairman of The Covey Leadership Center, a company engaged in leadership training and organizational development. He is the author of three national best-sellers,* The Seven Habits of Highly Effective People, Principle-Centered Leadership, *and* First Things First, *as well as* Spiritual Roots of Human Relations, How to Succeed with People, *and* The Divine Center.

The Anonymous Benefactor

SUSAN EASTON BLACK

WITH A CADILLAC, a maid, and a gardener, my family always had a Christmas with the best gifts from Santa's sleigh. The days my parents struggled to survive the Great Depression were only whispers of yesteryear when I was born. Mink had replaced wool and the country club societal whirl had captured my parents' fancy. In the 1950s they had become the American dream, and Christmas was merely an excuse to lavish each child with a fairyland of unrestrained wants.

My anticipation of opening gifts on Christmas Day was boundless, for I knew my mother was an uncontrolled shopper when it came to my whims. Being the only girl in a family of boys, I fared better than any at Christmas. My want list seemed to be surpassed only by my presents. After opening one gift after another, I toted my new acquisitions up and down the street so all the neighbors would know that Santa loved me best and that my parents were spoiling me to my complete satisfaction.

From such a worldly background of material prosperity, it seemed only natural for me to fantasize that when I had children of my own the established tradition of wealth and abundant giving at Christmas would continue—and that it would be even more lavish. If that had been the case, I would not have had one memorable Christmas—just more of the same. Stuffed animals may have been bigger and clothes fancier and gadgets more sophisticated, but ho-hum can be found even in the abundant life.

It was in 1977, almost twenty years ago, that my Christmas took a strange twist. Circumstances had changed. I was no longer the little girl awaiting the parental handout, but was an adult attempting to make my own way in life. I was a graduate student in 1977, completing a doctoral degree and raising three small sons alone. Like several other graduate students, I had obtained university employment as a research writer for a professor; and like most of the students, I was struggling to meet my financial obligations.

Having more "month than money" had become my norm, but never more so than in December 1977. Five days before Christmas, I realized that my mismanagement of funds would prevent any ostentation in gift buying for my children. In fact, it seemed to prevent much gift buying of any kind. It seemed unbearable to me—a young mother who knew all too well how to selfishly flaunt Christmas treasures before less fortunate neighbors, but not how to graciously be one of the less fortunate.

Cuddling my sons, I reluctantly explained my abhorrence of debt and the specter of our economic plight. My emotions surfaced as the children attempted to comfort me by nodding assuredly, "Don't worry! Santa Claus will give us gifts."

Cautiously I explained, "I think Santa Claus is also having a bad year."

With certainty my firstborn son, Brian, announced, "But on television his sleigh is still filled with toys. With five days left till Christmas, he'll have plenty for us." His younger brother Todd interjected, "Besides, Santa won't forget us. We've been good this year."

As all three nodded in agreement, I did too. My sons had been good. They had found happiness and friendship in our family; we all were unusually close. Perhaps it was our circumstance. Yet, despite their goodness, they would soon be disappointed because neither Santa nor mother would bring the desired presents on Christmas Day.

That night I cried and pled with the Lord for relief, for a glimmer of hope that Christmas in our home would be better than I anticipated. My verbal prayers awakened the children. They seemed to intuitively know what was causing my unhappiness. "Don't worry about presents. It doesn't matter," said Brian. I knew it

Cuddling my sons, I reluctantly explained the specter of our economic plight. My emotions surfaced as they attempted to comfort me by nodding assuredly, "Don't worry! Santa Claus will give us gifts."

didn't matter on December 20th, but I knew it would be *all*-important on December 25th.

The next morning I could not hide the despair and self-pity that had marred my face through the night. "What is wrong?" I was asked again and again at the university. My trite reply was "Nothing." Unconvinced friends pried and seemed in their own way to make matters worse. I snapped at the extended hand of friendship and grimaced at their undue interest in my personal life.

Arriving home, I methodically pulled the mail from the mailbox as I entered the house. A curious, unstamped envelope caught my attention. "To a very, very, very, very, very special lady" was typewritten on the envelope. I gazed at the envelope and wondered if it were meant for me. Hoping it was, I tore it open. To my surprise I found several dollars inside, but not a note of explanation.

"Come quickly," I beckoned my children. Together we counted the money, examined the envelope, and expressed wonder at the anonymous gift. This was a direct answer to my prayer. There was enough money in the envelope to buy an extra gift for each child. I was stunned and amazed, and my joy and excitement of Christmas had returned. It was going to be a great Christmas Day after all. It wouldn't be as lavish as those of my childhood, but it would be good enough.

I was curious. Where had the money come

Together we counted the money, examined the envelope, and expressed wonder at the anonymous gift. This was a direct answer to my prayer.

from? Could it be from a neighbor, a friend, a classmate, or the bishop? Logical deduction led me first to near neighbors. Visiting from house to house in our neighborhood proved embarrassing. As I attempted to thank neighbors, each stammered and then confessed, "It wasn't me." Calling friends and thanking them elicited clever expressions. "If you find out who is giving away money, tell them to send some my way." Classmates rendered similar comments.

It must be the bishop, I decided. He knew what I paid in tithing and would be aware that a less than exciting Christmas would be awaiting my family. The children and I walked to his house and knocked on the door. Enthusiastically, we thanked him for his generosity. However, he denied being our benefactor and assured us that he did not know who had been so kind.

Curiosity mounted as nightfall approached. I read the envelope again: "To a very, very, very, very, very special lady." This time I noticed that the "e" and "l" were misshapen letters produced by an old typewriter ribbon. I also observed that each dollar bill had been folded and unfolded many times, as if each one had been of infinite worth. My desire to discover the identity of the anonymous donor grew. Soon that desire was coupled with the gnawing resolve to return the money. The misshapen letters and folded dollar bills evidenced that the generous donor also had financial difficulties.

I couldn't sleep that night. Again and again I

asked myself, "Who was it?" I had the clues of the old typewriter ribbon and the folded money, but not the answer. I can't really describe how I finally knew who the benefactor was, but about two o'clock in the morning, I knew. I knew who had a broken typewriter, and who needed to replace their ribbon, and who carefully folded and unfolded money, checking each dollar bill. It was my three sons.

My desire to discover the identity of the anonymous donor grew. Soon that desire was coupled with the gnawing resolve to return the money. Obviously the generous donor also had financial difficulties.

With tears of love, I awoke the donors. Blurry-eyed they asked, "What's wrong?" I replied, "Nothing's wrong; everything is right! You gave me the money. You gave me all the money you possess!" Opening the bedroom closet door, I pulled out three empty jars that once had contained their treasured fortune. They sat silent for several moments until my nine-year-old Brian turned to his younger brother Todd and punched him. "You told!" he exclaimed. Attempting to fend off further blows, Todd yelled, "It wasn't me, it must have been John." Their five-year-old brother immediately said, "It wasn't me," as both boys landed on him. In unison they asked, "How did you know?"

I had searched outside my home for the answer—but the answer was within. I had seen generosity in all those around me, but had failed to recognize the generous hearts of my children. And now I more clearly knew why the Savior had said, "Suffer the little children to come unto me, and forbid them not: for of such is the kingdom of [heaven]." (Mark 10:14; Luke 18:16.) My house, with all of its material flaws, was my

heaven on earth, and my sons were my greatest treasure. Christmas 1977 was indeed a merry Christmas worth remembering.

SUSAN EASTON BLACK *is professor of Church history and doctrine and associate dean of general education and honors at Brigham Young University. She is the author of* Finding Christ through the Book of Mormon *and the editor of* Lion of the Lord: Essays on the Life and Service of Brigham Young *and* The Prophet Joseph: Essays on the Life and Mission of Joseph Smith. *A brief version of this article appeared as "The Envelope," in* Latter-day Digest, *vol. 2, no. 3, pp. 27–29.*

Silent Substitute

ANNE OSBORN POELMAN

MEMORIES ARE QUIRKY. They can be annoyingly elusive, slipping just beyond our grasp as we vainly try to retrieve some errant thought. They can also be disturbingly evocative, bringing with them a cascade of thoughts and feelings that may momentarily overwhelm present reality.

Memory is also a type of Orwellian time machine: Step into it and years are erased instantaneously as it transports us from the Now into the Back When. Stir in the intense emotions that surround special times and events. Spice memory up with a dollop of nostalgia. Toss in a bit of the child that secretly dwells in all of us. The result? A potent brew that can inspire or depress us, excite or calm us, satisfy or shame us, comfort or disturb us.

Christmas. The very word evokes a flood of memories along with the hope of future salvation.

Christmas. A time for giving. Also a time for rampant greed.

Christmas. A time for family. Also a time that can accentuate loneliness and heartache.

Christmas. A time for joy. Also a time of uncertainty for those who give. Will the offering be accepted? Will it be enough? Or will it be rejected with a disappointed, "Is that all?"

Christmas. For newlyweds, the first big holiday. A time to revel in newfound relationships. A time to plan painstakingly for the perfect gift that will surely surprise and delight a loved one. A time of unspoken anxiety, too: How will we blend two sets of traditions, two sets of expectations? And, yes, two sets of memories.

As our first Christmas together approached, Ron and I somewhat gingerly approached the topic of the impending holiday.

"So," I asked, carefully choosing a neutral subject. "About Christmas. Are there any sorts of special things to eat that you particularly liked?"

Ron chuckled.

"Of course! We didn't have much money when I was growing up and couldn't afford the fancy stuff. But I do remember one Christmas when my mother made Scottish shortbread. I thought it was the best thing I'd ever tasted. Talk about 'melt in your mouth'! I think it took a whole pound of butter. So she only made it once," he concluded wistfully.

I silently resolved to search every cookbook in the cupboard for a basic shortbread recipe, modify it, and then surprise him with a batch.

"What about you?" he returned.

"I was really a very finicky eater. So I mostly remember what I *didn't* like."

He persisted. "Well, what was it?"

I groaned in mock despair. "Rutabagas! And scalloped oysters!"

"Ugh!" We both made faces and vowed to eliminate those two noisome items from the menu.

Ron grew reflective.

"So what is your most memorable Christmas? Aside from the one we're about to have," he added hastily.

"I suppose it's the time we went to Kansas City to visit Baba and Bill—Mom's parents. I was only six. We drove to Chicago a few days before Christmas and got on the Burlington overnight train to Kansas City. We had two adjoining bedrooms in the sleeper car; each had an upper and a lower berth. Lucy and I shared one; Mom and Dad and the baby—Greg—shared the other.

"I got the upper berth," I continued with a satisfied smile. "Lucy was younger, so they put her in the lower berth. We kids were already dressed in our pajamas when we left Culver, so we went right to bed. I was so excited I thought I'd never get to sleep. But once the train pulled out of Dearborn Street Station, the rhythmic swaying of the cars and the monotonous clackety-clack of the wheels put me right into never-never land.

"When we woke up, we were nearly there. Kansas City's Union Station! It was almost magical. You know: going to sleep one place and waking up in an entirely different one. We had breakfast in the dining car. Pancakes with gooey syrup and lots of butter!" I mentally smacked my lips at the delicious memory.

Ron was momentarily silent. I looked at him expectantly, then it hit me. Traveling on the train—*any* train—would have been a rare occurrence for the Poelman family. Sleeping berths and tasty meals in the dining car? An unheard-of luxury.

I felt a rush of shame at my insensitivity.

"So," I asked sheepishly, attempting to deflect attention from my gaffe, "what was *your* most special Christmas?"

Surprisingly, his face brightened. "Oddly enough, my most memorable Christmas was when I was sixteen. The Depression was over—at least officially. But many families such as ours still struggled with its lingering aftereffects. Dad had often been out of work. He and Mom were really anxious about Christmas, knowing there was just enough money for food and other basic necessities. Little—if any—would be left for presents."

Ron shook his head ruefully at the memory of his parents' dilemma.

"I asked my parents if they would let me be the Santa Claus this Christmas. Mom and Dad were reluctant to accept but grateful. So they agreed."

"They talked with us all, trying to prepare us for a skimpy Christmas. Suddenly, the thought struck me: *I* could be Santa Claus! Or at least his silent substitute! I'd been working every day after school to help out and I'd managed to save a bit extra. So I asked my parents if they would let me be the Santa Claus this Christmas. I could provide the gifts for my younger brothers and sisters! Without the kids knowing who did it, of course."

He grinned happily. "Mom and Dad were reluctant to accept but grateful. So they agreed.

"I was really excited! I counted my savings and planned really carefully. First I allocated some money for the tree, which Dad always decorated with painstaking care. With great ceremony, he would drape each individual silver icicle and tinsel over its branches until the whole tree shimmered!

"I bought a pretty sweater for teenaged Carol. Toys for Stuart and baby Keith. My younger brother Lloyd was only ten at the time. He didn't talk about it much, but I knew in his heart of hearts he longed for a bicycle. I couldn't afford a brand-new one, so I took my old one to Eldredge's bicycle shop and had them put new tires and pedals on it. They polished and repainted it, put new grips on the handlebars. It looked terrific!

"I could hardly wait, but Christmas Eve finally came. After the kids were in bed, I helped Mom and Dad put the gifts under the tree. I was singing in the East High A Capella Choir and we had a special carol service later that night in the old Douglas Ward. I had some very intense feelings as we sang hymns and listened to the Christmas story read from the book of Luke."

His eyes moistened at the memory.

"When we came outside after the concert was over, it had started to snow. A glistening white frosting coated every branch of every tree. It had an almost magical quality. I walked home alone, wanting to treasure and savor those special feelings. I think I realized, perhaps for the first time, what the real spirit of Christmas is. Being the secret giver filled me with gratitude to our Heavenly Father for his own gift to us, the Savior Jesus Christ.

"Christmas morning, I quietly watched my brothers and sisters come into the living room. Their joy at the unexpected gifts was reward enough. Later on that day I realized—to my own surprise and delight—that I hadn't once thought about what gifts *I* might receive!

"That," he concluded, "was my most memorable Christmas. I guess it still is."

Tears ran down my cheeks as I imagined the teenaged Ron walking home in the snow, heart filled to overflowing with the joy of giving. It even made me a tiny bit envious, knowing that the kind of sacrifices he and his family made for each other bonded them in a way that even the most closely knit but better-off families may not experience.

Fast forward a few years. Now comfortable with

"I think I realized, perhaps for the first time, what the real spirit of Christmas is. Being the secret giver filled me with gratitude to our Heavenly Father for his own gift to us, the Savior Jesus Christ."

each other's traditions and having invented a few new ones of our own, Ron and I relished the Christmas holidays. One of my favorite Poelman traditions was the annual Christmas family home evening.

This particular year we gathered at Lloyd and Catherine's home for a potluck supper and evening program. By the time all the brothers and sisters, in-laws, children, married cousins and *their* children, plus a few guests had squeezed in, the house was quite literally packed to the rafters. Happy chatter filled the family room. A blazing fire crackled away merrily, adding to the festivity.

After supper was over, Lloyd called the clan together. Following his brief welcoming remarks, a Christmas hymn and prayer started the much-anticipated family home evening. Then Lloyd stood again.

"This year I thought we might do things a bit differently. Instead of a program, it occurred to us that the children might be interested to hear their parents, aunts, and uncles talk about their most memorable Christmases. Okay?"

After nods of assent, Lloyd suggested that Ron—as the oldest—begin first. Somewhat diffidently, Ron told the gathering about that long-ago post-Depression Christmas. Mostly, he spoke about how he *felt*.

The children listened raptly, murmuring their empathy.

"After dinner, we each opened our single gift that was under the tree. Pajamas, of course. I tried not to cry as we hugged each other and said 'Merry Christmas' as we went off to bed."

Each of the brothers and sisters spoke in turn. As the host, Lloyd spoke last.

Obviously struggling with his feelings, Lloyd cleared his throat and began.

"I didn't know about Ron's role in that Christmas. I, too, feel that was my most memorable Christmas. I was only ten years old at the time. Old enough to feel the concern and anxiety of my parents; too young to understand the constant worry of providing for a large family in those difficult times."

He paused, overcome by memories. A faraway expression swept across his face. When he resumed, it was as though ten-year-old Lloyd Poelman was talking.

You could have heard a pin drop in that crowded room. All eyes were fixed on Lloyd as he continued.

"I had a secret wish that Christmas. More than I'd ever wanted anything, I wanted a bicycle. It was an impossible dream. Something that was so far beyond reason I scarcely dared even think about it, let alone hope for it.

"Christmas Eve came. After dinner, we each opened our single gift that was under the tree. Pajamas, of course. It always was; Mom and Dad had to make a practical necessity into a gift. I tried not to cry as we hugged each other and said 'Merry Christmas' as we went off to bed."

The ten-year-old Lloyd's face was bleak as he

struggled bravely to keep his disappointment from showing.

"Dad always got up first on Christmas morning. He would stoke the fire and turn the tree lights on. Then, and only then, were we allowed to come into the living room. I knew in my heart of hearts that Santa hadn't come. The floor under the tree would be as barren as it had been the night before. But I wanted to be a 'good scout,' so I straightened up my new pajamas and trooped in with the rest.

"And when I walked in, I rubbed my eyes in disbelief. There—*there,* right under the tree—was the biggest, most beautiful shiny bicycle I'd ever seen! And it had a great big tag on it that just said, 'LLOYD'!"

He gulped back a sob, his voice still thick with wonder. There wasn't a dry eye as everyone crowded around to hug Lloyd. Hug each other. Hug anyone in the room, for that matter. Forty plus years later, Lloyd's story created an unforgettable Christmas for our entire family. We still talk about it, one of our most cherished Christmas memories.

(P.S. In case you want the shortbread recipe, here it is. It's been called "to die for." Maybe it is, given the cholesterol that lurks in every bite.)

"I knew in my heart of hearts that Santa hadn't come. The floor under the tree would be as barren as it had been the night before. But I wanted to be a 'good scout,' so I straightened up my new pajamas and trooped in with the rest."

ANNIE'S SHORTBREADS

Cream together:

- **1 C** granulated white sugar
- **1 C** butter (the better the quality, the better the product)

Add **3 C** unbleached white flour.

Roll out on a cookie sheet to about 3/8" thickness. Chill in refrigerator until moderately firm. Score dough with a knife into squares. Prick each square with a fork. Chill again until quite firm. Cut along scored lines into squares. Separate squares and place about 1/2" apart on cookie sheets.

Bake in oven preheated to **275°F**. Remove when squares barely begin to turn golden brown around the edges. Cool completely on racks.

Store in tightly covered container. Frozen, they'll last for several weeks. That is, unless the two-legged mice get into them first!

ANNE OSBORN POELMAN *is professor of radiology at the University of Utah School of Medicine and is the first occupant of the William H. and Patricia N. Child Presidential Endowed Chair Honoring Pioneering Utah Women in Medicine. She is the 1996 recipient of the Rosenblatt Prize, given annually to honor the top faculty member at the University of Utah. An internationally renowned lecturer, Anne travels extensively to share her medical expertise in neuroradiology (the diagnosis of brain and spine diseases). She has written a number of medical textbooks; The Simeon Solution is her first book for a general audience. Anne and her husband, Elder Ronald E. Poelman of the First Quorum of the Seventy, live in Salt Lake City.*

Long-Lasting Battery

DEAN HUGHES

When Santa Claus gave me my first bicycle, he left it on the front porch. When I didn't find it by the tree, where I expected it, I had to fight back the tears. But I was all the happier when, after some broad hints, I stepped outside and discovered it—in all its shiny splendor. That was a magical year. But it is not my favorite Christmas memory.

I also think fondly of the first year Kathy and I were married, when I shopped and shopped to find just the right things for her. And I remember some of those wonderful years when our kids were young: like the year little Tom got walkie-talkies and we spent the afternoon trying to think of things to say: "Can you hear me? Over." "Yes, I hear you. Over." "Okay. Over." But those years are still not my favorites. My most treasured memory involves something much more prosaic: a car battery.

Kathy and I were living in Seattle in 1967. It was our second Christmas as a married couple. I was in my first year of graduate school at the University of Washington, and Kathy was teaching at a high school. She was pregnant, however, and she was planning to stop working in the middle of the year. She was making the fabulous salary of $5,900 a year, but all that was soon going to stop, and we had accumulated very little in savings—all of which had to go toward my next tuition. We were trying to squeeze our budget to the absolute limit, and that meant that Christmas had to be *very* simple, so we shopped wisely for our families ("cheaply" is probably the more accurate word), and we agreed to give each other almost nothing.

Kathy was in desperate need of clothes, and I had bought her a psychedelic maternity dress that was ugly even by the standards of the sixties. (For some reason, it was on sale.) She had made herself a couple of outfits, and she had to get by with just those few options. There was simply no more blood in the turnip.

One day Kathy was cooking a pot of chili for a ward dinner, and she sent me to buy some of the ingredients. One of the items was "one large onion." At the grocery store, I happened to discover the largest onion I had ever seen—the size of a cantaloupe—and I thought it would be funny to bring it home. But it cost 38 cents. I debated, and then decided to splurge. Well, we both laughed, and we still joke about that "one large onion," but the point is, I really gave the expense serious thought. We were trying to get by on ten dollars a week for groceries, and 38 cents was a fair hunk of that.

Kathy would take the car to school each day. I carpooled with some students in our apartment building. And, by the way, our apartment was a real dump. The bathroom was filled with disgusting aromas, and poor Kathy, with morning sickness, would have to face that chamber of horrors every day. But one snowy morning about a week before Christmas, she held her breath long enough to get ready and then walked out to the car, turned the ignition key, and got no response. She somehow found a ride to school, but I was left to see what I could do about the car.

In the next little while I checked around for some jumper cables and found none. I was in a hurry because I had a class that morning, and so I came up with the idea of removing the battery, carrying it to a nearby gas station, and leaving it to be charged. All was going well with that plan until I was striding down the street and slipped on some ice. As I swan-dived toward the sidewalk, I tried to keep the battery from landing first. I hammered my elbows, but still the sacrifice was not enough: the battery struck the pavement. I thought it was all right for a moment, but then I saw a crack in the casing.

I can still remember how ill I felt at that moment. My bruised elbows would heal themselves, but a battery is less resilient. I was quite certain the thing wouldn't take a charge now, and I was running out of time, so I decided I better catch my ride to school and worry about the car later.

What a day I had! I concluded that I would have to buy a new battery, and I estimated the cost at about twenty-five dollars. But it might as well have been twenty-five hundred. We simply didn't have any extra money. Even worse was knowing that it was my fault and I would have to tell Kathy what a dumb thing I'd done. You have to understand that I'm not usually a klutz about falling down, but when it comes to mechanical things, I was—and am—a poor excuse for a "provider." I never felt it more than I did that day.

Somewhere in the course of that morning, however, I thought of Don Gessel. Don and his wife, Elaine, had more or less adopted us at the time we had arrived in Seattle. We knew a relative of theirs in Ogden—and with no more motivation than that, the Gessels began to invite us to dinner and to look after us. On a few occasions Don had kept our dear old Mercury Comet operating. He had once worked as an auto mechanic, and he had all the right equipment in his garage. Out of pity for our financial plight, he had repaired our car and charged us only the price of the parts.

It's important to understand Don. He was wonderfully helpful, but he could also be rather—well, "gruff" is too strong a word and "terse" sounds a little too sophisticated. He was certainly "direct." And he asked those questions my dad had always posed: "How

I concluded that I would have to buy a new battery, and I estimated the cost at about twenty-five dollars. But it might as well have been twenty-five hundred. We simply didn't have any extra money.

long have you been running around on that low tire? You're going to ruin it."

I would look at the tire with considerable surprise and mumble that I was sure it must have gone down overnight—since I tried to be careful about such things. But in my heart of hearts, I knew that I rarely thought to check.

"Don't you ever change your oil?" "Do you know you have a tail-light out?" These were hard questions for me, however appropriate, and I was always afraid of people like my dad—and Don—who asked me such things. All the same, I decided to call Don when I got home that day. Maybe there was some way to patch a cracked battery, or maybe a crack didn't matter all that much—as long as nothing leaked out. What did I know? I only knew that Don would know.

I had to break the news to Kathy that night, and she was as sick as I was—but nice about it. And then I called Don. "It's probably shot," he told me, "but bring it out and I'll try to give it a charge." The problem was, I had no way to get it to his house. "Well, I'll tell you what," he said. "I think I've got a battery that might fit your car. I'll drive over and put it in, and you can get by with that for now. Then I'll see how bad you smashed up your own battery."

When he arrived, he teased me a little about the nosedive I had taken, but otherwise he was pretty lenient on a guy who had done something that stupid. I told him I would come out the next night and check on the battery. "You're coming out for Christmas dinner, aren't you?" he asked, and I told him we were. "Well, don't worry about it until then." So that gave me a few days—a little reprieve before I had to figure out a way to come up with the money that we didn't have.

Have you ever prayed for a car battery? I prayed for a sump pump once, in the middle of a terrible storm, and the pump was healed. But that was later. Even back then, however, I had no doubt that God could make that battery well, and I could think of no other way to solve the problem. I was certainly better at praying than I was at fixing, and so I prayed every day until Christmas that somehow a miracle would happen. By the time I walked into the Gessels' home on Christmas Day, I was saying silent prayers and hoping to hear that my faith had softened and welded that plastic casing. But I had not been there a full minute before Don said, "That battery of yours is *dead*. It wouldn't take a charge."

I felt my stomach turn over. I didn't have time to think what to do, but I remember how completely desolate I felt. God had turned down all my requests.

And then Don said, "Just keep that battery that's in your car. That'll be your Christmas present."

This was the miracle. My battery wasn't healed, but I was.

For a few seconds, I couldn't get a word out, but when I found my voice, I tried to thank him. But Don didn't like my gushing; he brushed it off and changed

Have you ever prayed for a car battery? I had no doubt that God could make that battery well. I prayed every day until Christmas that somehow a miracle would happen.

the subject. I guess you could say he was "terse" about it.

Kathy and I have been trying to thank Don and Elaine—and the Lord—ever since. We try, especially at Christmas, to notice someone—a student or a family going through a hard time—and give them some anonymous help. Once we even had a chance to buy a young friend a new battery. But we never feel that we have done enough to pay the debt—not even close.

It took me a while to realize that I had actually received what I prayed for. My battery took a charge after all—one that has lasted all these years—even though my casing is dreadfully full of cracks.

DEAN HUGHES *is a full-time author who has written more than sixty children's books, including the popular Lucky Ladd series. With his son Tom, he has written* Great Stories from Mormon History *and* We'll Bring the World His Truth.

"Losing the Christmas Spirit"

MARION D. HANKS

ARREN BAINBRIDGE was an able and amiable gentleman, much in the pattern of other respectfully remembered pastors of established religious groups who over the years have been recruited to serve congregations in our predominantly Mormon area. I became acquainted with this choice man through attendance at a weekly meeting of a service group to which we both belonged. We grew to be good friends, and I developed strong affection for him. He was a devoted leader of a large Protestant congregation, and his members, I learned from many reports, greatly appreciated their minister.

"It was not his preaching," one of them explained, "though he was a fine preacher. It was not his counseling skills, though he was a trusted, qualified counselor. It was his love for us! He really loved us, and we quickly learned to love him."

Our first three daughters were very young and the other two children not yet born when the Bainbridges moved from our city to another state to conclude his distinguished career among family and friends there. Over the years they continued occasional contact with us, with particular attention to our eldest daughter, Susan, who was about four when we had a special experience with Dr. Bainbridge. The effects of that occasion endure still with our family, for us like a sparkling Christmas candle lighting a path of memory and motivation in our neighborhood and community and beyond.

It has seemed remarkable to us that no Christmas season in all the passing years has come and gone without recurring tender memories of the Christmas Day worship service our family attended at the Methodist Church where Reverend Bainbridge ministered. The celebration of Christ's advent fell on Sunday that year, and my wife and I decided that after attending our own morning services we would join Warren's congregation to share with our little ones the experience of worshiping with another admired church group on this special day.

It was a decision and a privilege we have rejoiced in through all the intervening years.

We arrived at the downtown church just before the meeting began and were cordially welcomed by assigned greeters at the door. We had not notified Reverend Bainbridge of our coming, desiring to join his group as worshipers rather than as special guests. By the time we arrived at the entrance to the sanctuary he had left his place at the door of the chapel, perhaps to enjoy a few moments of quiet thought and prayer in preparation for the services which he would conduct and preach.

As the meeting began, the Hanks family cheerily joined with members of the congregation as we sang together treasured Christian hymns and stood in the responsive reading of familiar scriptures pertinent to the holy season.

For our children and for us it was a delightful, different, and very enjoyable experience. These many years later our daughters recall and appreciate that good day when we broadened our feeling for and understanding of other people and other ways of worship.

But the heart and highlight of our adventure that Sabbath morning was yet—and soon—to come. The Reverend Dr. Warren Bainbridge approached the lectern to deliver his Christmas message. The congregation stirred in anticipation of this seasoned platform speaker's holiday sermon. He looked first to the right, then to the left to recognize the large congregation, then briefly to the notes on his pulpit, and began his sermon.

The dynamic teacher had no trouble arresting the full attention of the Hanks family that day with his first words: "My dear friend, Elder Marion D. Hanks," he began, "a General Authority of The Church of Jesus

The congregation stirred in anticipation of their pastor's holiday sermon. He looked first to the right, then to the left to recognize the large congregation, then briefly to his notes, and began his sermon.

Startled and adjusting his glasses, he blurted, "Elder Hanks, is that you?" Assured that it was I, he continued, wonderingly leaning over the pulpit, "And is that Mrs. Hanks and your children? Could that be Susan sitting by you?"

Christ of Latter-day Saints, shared with me this week a tender family story with which I would like to begin my message today.

"Susan, the eldest of the three little girls then in the Hanks family, awakened in the night 'upchucking,' as her daddy said, perhaps from a slight overdose of holiday excitement and anticipation mingled with the season's largess of goodies. Rocking in her father's comforting arms, Susan looked up into his eyes and said, 'Daddy, for awhile I thought I was losing the Christmas Spirit.'"

At that moment in his sermon Warren Bainbridge looked full into the faces of those filling the center section of pews, anticipating with a smile the gentle murmurs of appreciative response that came from the congregation.

And also at that moment the pastor's eyes fell on my face. Startled and adjusting his glasses, he blurted, "Elder Hanks, is that you?" Assured that it was I, he continued, wonderingly leaning over the pulpit, "And is that Mrs. Hanks and your children? Could that be Susan sitting by you?" He had our family stand to be recognized and then offered, with tears, a warm and loving expression of appreciation and incredulity that we were there to worship with him and his people in his church on Christmas Day. It seemed to him a thing incredible that a Mormon leader and his family would come and join in celebrating with them during this holiday season the faith we shared and our loving appreciation for the Savior.

He told me later that to his knowledge his church had never had such a visit before. It was not with such thought in mind that we had made the decision to be with Brother Bainbridge and his people. I had come to know the man and his character and integrity, so when the unique opportunity presented itself, we went with no agenda other than to manifest our love for him and for the Master whom he had served with earnest sincerity over a lifetime.

I have thought much on that day since. Perhaps in this generation it would seem less unusual for such an event to occur. Under direction of Church leaders, and often involving members of the First Presidency, there now seems to be a much more intensive intermingling with leaders of other denominations, including a not infrequent joint involvement in serving the indigent, needy, and suffering people in our community and the world. Many Church members express delight in this development.

Community service activity and outreach by Latter-day Saint missionaries across the earth, and widespread participation in Christian service by local Church units and individuals, have made a difference in the perception of our religion by others. Many have not understood the Christ-centered theology and earnest application of Christ's instruction and example which are the foundation of the Church and its people.

For us, nothing is more fundamental in our faith than the truth that God is the loving Father of all mankind, and that the "first and great commandment, and the second like unto it" (upon which two commandments all other teachings of the law and the prophets hang) are that we are to love him with everything in us, and to love our neighbor as ourselves. *Christ died for all mankind,* and as a commitment to him and as an element of our religious faith, we must look for and respond to the needs of those about us. As children of God, loving him, *we have all his other children as our neighbors, and we have been enjoined to love and serve them.* The scriptures teach that our salvation and our happiness depend as much on how we treat other human beings as upon anything else. It is the *kind of people we are* that really matters; indeed, *this is the test of how well we have understood and internalized all that we believe to be true.*

For many years, our young Latter-day Saint missionary representatives have given selfless, significant service in the refugee camps of Southeast Asia. Without exception, they have come out of that difficult, dangerous undertaking saying, "This is the most decent thing I have ever done; my life will never be the same again." Faithfully keeping United Nations camp rules, which appropriately restrained denominational instruction from various faith groups and agencies serving in the refugee camps, our representatives taught no missionary discussions, but they accepted the opportunity and responsibility to prepare the refugees to speak English as a second language and to provide the cultural orientation that would qualify them to be received in a third country. Our young people have done the work of Christ and are receiving the pay of Christ. In the peace and pleasantness of their own consciences, they have received the warm spiritual assurance that in service to these, "the least of these [his] brethren," they truly were serving him. (See Matt. 25:40.)

And there have been wonderful outcomes to this honest, patient procedure. One unforgettable and memorable incident symbolizing the sweetness of service in the sobering atmosphere of the refugee camps occurred one Christmas. Our wonderful young lady representatives had presented a Christmas pageant in music and drama telling the story of Mary and Joseph and the Christ Child to a large group of refugees, many of whom had never before heard of it. A refugee mother, with wonder in her eyes and voice, approached the lovely missionary who had represented Mary, mother of Christ, holding a tiny brown baby in her arms representing the Savior, and said, "Why, the story of Mary and Joseph and Jesus is a *refugee* story, isn't it!"

Joseph Smith once wrote, "*A man filled with the love of God, is not content with blessing his family alone, but ranges through the whole world, anxious to bless the whole human race.*" (Joseph Smith, *History of The Church of Jesus Christ of Latter-day Saints*, 2d ed., 7 vols. [Salt Lake City: The Church of Jesus Christ of

A refugee mother, with wonder in her eyes and voice, approached the lovely missionary who had represented Mary, mother of Christ, and said, "Why, the story of Mary and Joseph and Jesus is a refugee story, isn't it!"

Latter-day Saints, 1951], 4:227.) On another occasion he said, *"We are to feed the hungry, to clothe the naked, to provide for the widow, to dry up the tear of the orphan, to comfort the afflicted, whether in this church, or in any other, or in no church at all, wherever [we] find them."* (*Times and Seasons,* March 15, 1842, p. 732.)

In 1978 the First Presidency issued an official statement regarding the position of The Church of Jesus Christ of Latter-day Saints toward other religions. A concluding paragraph reads: *"Our message . . . is one of special love and concern for the eternal welfare of all men and women, regardless of religious belief, race, or nationality, knowing that we are truly brothers and sisters because we are the sons and daughters of the same eternal Father."*

Our family has been blessed in the remembrance of a Christmas that included worshiping with our friend and neighbors in another church. The surprised delight he and they expressed because we were there out of love and caring has inspired us and our extended family and motivated other, similar undertakings through the years.

ELDER MARION D. HANKS *was sustained as a member of the First Council of the Seventy in 1953. He served in a number of positions as a General Authority, including twice as a member of the Presidency of the First Quorum of the Seventy, from 1953 until 1992, when he was given emeritus status. He is the author of* A Warm and Gracious Christmas *and* Gifts from a Mother.

"The Lights Are On"

BARBARA W. WINDER

THE SPRING AFTER the Berlin Wall fell, my husband, Richard W. Winder, and I were called to reopen the Czechoslovakia Mission. (It has since become the Czech/Slovak Mission.) As we filled this responsibility, words from the hymn "Hark, All Ye Nations!" sank deep into my heart:

> Searching in darkness, nations have wept;
> Watching for dawn, their vigil they've kept.
> All now rejoice; the long night is o'er.
> Truth is on earth once more!
> Oh, how glorious from the throne above
> Shines the gospel light of truth and love!
> Bright as the sun, this heavenly ray
> Lights ev'ry land today.

Soon after we arrived, I found myself praying for relief from the dismal sadness I felt all around me. I noticed many downcast eyes as I passed people on our morning walk to the near-empty grocery store. My smile and "Good morning" to the people who were now becoming familiar fell silent to the ground. Also, the sight of run-down buildings left from forty years of communist neglect added to my gloom. Surely this constant state of disrepair took its toll on the Czech people as well. And so I prayed for them, too. Gradually, blessed relief came. It came as I learned about the innate goodness of these people, and their love of beauty and creativity.

One friendship began as we waited in line at the drugstore. We were practicing how to express ourselves in Czech when a lovely young lawyer, Suzana Otcenaskova, who spoke beautiful English, asked how she could help us, then kindly ordered for us. A newly converted microbiologist, Alena Pichova, took her precious time to acquaint us with the city, its history, and its culture—she even kept us posted on current events. Anything we needed to know, Alena could help us. She was our walking encyclopedia. There were only a few longtime members of the Church in the country. They willingly shared their expertise.

Our evening walk to an overlook where we could see the outline of Saint Vitus Cathedral on the horizon, and the slow, meandering Vltava River below, took us through our neighborhood. On the way we admired the neighbors' gardens. We stopped to talk to Mr. Oldrich Petronek about his roses. He had many varieties which were large and beautiful. At our first comment of admiration, he snipped a beautiful bouquet and placed it into our hands. Oldrich and his enthusiastic wife, Marie, though twenty years younger than we, became our benefactors on many occasions. Their teenage children, Lenka and Olda, came to our home to learn English, and we practiced our Czech language skills with them. They were like our family.

Our spirits were continually lifted, not only because of the love and goodness shown to us by many wonderful people, but also because of the beauty of the Czech countryside. The soft, green rolling hills bordered by dark evergreens were refreshing on warm summer days. With the onset of fall the fields took on harvest hues, with the deciduous trees dressed in brilliant colors backed by the patches of deep-shaded evergreens. When winter came the fields looked soft under their blanket of snow. Warmly dressed skaters frolicked to and fro over the frozen ponds, with a backdrop of frosted trees and wisps of smoke curling from the farmhouse chimneys.

It was Thanksgiving time. I was grateful that my prayers were being answered. There was beauty everywhere, and dear people were so kind to adopt us, strangers in their country. Then the Christmas season was upon us. We were fascinated with their traditions and willing to share some of our own. We began to wonder where to get a Christmas tree. We asked neighbors Marie and Oldrich. "Not to worry" was their reply. The very next day a Christmas tree appeared on our

Try as we might, we could not find lights. Occasionally, we saw a candle in a window, or there might be a tiny birthday candle in an empty walnut shell. Was the light of Christ really so tiny here?

porch! We found the Czech traditional corn-husk angels in a town near Slovakia and tied them onto the tree with red crochet thread. Try as we might, we could not find lights. That was quite all right; no one seemed to have lights. Occasionally, we saw a candle in a window, or there might be a tiny birthday candle in an empty walnut shell. Was the light of Christ really so tiny here?

Saint Nicholas Day is December 6. Three personages visit the homes of children on that day: an angel, a devil, and Saint Nicholas, who is not the plump, jolly old elf we are accustomed to, but a rather slender, saintly man, dressed in a long red cloak trimmed with white fur. If a child has been bad the devil shakes his chains and growls, and of course gives no gift. However, if the child has been good then a gift is left by the angel.

There were beautiful nativities everywhere, made of wood, corn husks, ceramic, gingerbread, or papier-mâché. Each is adored for its degree of creativity. Our Church lawyer, Dr. Josef Radil, and his wife, Eve, took us and their two young sons to tour some of the famous nativities in Prague on Christmas Day. We also visited the Saint Vitus Cathedral and heard the choir singing in the balcony high above us. With no heat in the building, the choir was bundled in their warmest clothing. It was amazing how they could stay on pitch in such a low temperature. We and the Radil family warmed ourselves afterward in our living quarters with our family's traditional Christmas brunch.

With no heat in the building, the choir was bundled in their warmest clothing. It was amazing how they could stay on pitch in such a low temperature.

We wanted to show our gratitude to our helpful neighbors. So we gathered the local missionaries and Dr. Radil's family to prepare treats to take caroling. This was new and different for Czech people, but we and our treats were warmly received. At the home of a recently widowed neighbor, Mrs. Francova, we began with an American song familiar to the Czechs, "Jingle Bells." She and her two teenage sons bobbed up and down with the rhythm. We then sang a couple of Czech carols and started to close with a carol we share in common, the German-originated "Silent Night." Mrs. Francova melted into tears and fell into my arms sobbing. Her heart was softened and she allowed her sons to receive the missionary lessons.

A Czech Christmas custom particularly fascinating to us was the harvesting and selling of Christmas carp. Early in December, carp were brought into the towns and cities from the numerous countryside ponds. Carp tanks appeared on the street corners about two weeks before Christmas, usually near grocery stores where housewives could easily buy their fish. The merchant, clad in warm clothing, heavy rubber boots, and a long rubber apron, watched as the customer selected her fish from among the others swimming in the tanks. In a quick motion the net would capture the desired one. Then, just as quickly, the head was hit and the fish was cleaned right before our eyes.

Sometimes the carp was purchased alive, to be taken home in a water-filled plastic bag. It would live in the family bathtub until preparation time. Dr. Radil's family chose this method. However, they always purchased two carp, a large one for Christmas dinner and a small one to be taken back to the countryside and slipped into the pond. This seemed to dispel the boys' grief over the dead fish and helped them enjoy their Christmas dinner a little better. Christmas dinner is always carp soup, followed by fried or baked carp with potato salad, and completed with plates of dainty cookies.

Christmas Eve is the most sacred time of the season for the Czech/Slovak people. This time is reserved for the family. It is the time of gift exchange, a time to share the closeness of dear ones.

Josef Podlipny, president of the Prague District, was aware we would be holding interviews with the missionaries on Christmas Eve. He and his wife, Jirina, invited us to have dinner with them. We declined, not wanting to interfere with their family customs. President Podlipny persisted. So, compromising, we said we would stop by in the early afternoon to wish them a Merry Christmas and deliver some treats for the children.

After the final missionary interview, it was still early enough in the day that we could make it to the Podlipnys' without disturbing their family time. They must have been watching for us, since we had barely rung the bell when we were greeted by eleven-year-old Martin, scrubbed and dressed in his Sunday suit, and thirteen-year-old Lea, looking like an angel in her soft white dress. The children possessed an air of excitement

We had barely rung the bell when we were greeted by eleven-year-old Martin, scrubbed and dressed in his Sunday suit, and thirteen-year-old Lea, looking like an angel in her soft white dress.

as they helped us put on the customary slippers and as we greeted Josef and Jirina. A beautifully set table with fresh flowers filled the center of the living room, and the Christmas tree, artistically adorned with traditional Czech ornaments, was near the balcony window. Josef's and Jirina's parents were also present. Barely had we been introduced and exchanged greetings when we were given places of honor at the dinner table. They wanted us with them at this sacred family time! They had moved their dinner to afternoon, completely surprising us and engulfing us with their love. During our shared time, we felt the care and concern of the grandparents, not yet members, for their grandchildren, who were so different in their social habits and beliefs from other children. "Would they be accepted and have friends?" they worried. We felt the generations bridged by the love and respect Josef and Jirina displayed for their parents. The story of the first Christmas was read aloud from Luke, and we joined together in singing Czech Christmas carols. We rejoiced in this beautiful family, their goodness, their faithful example, and their kindness to us. Our hearts were filled with love—the Spirit of Christmas!

Two years passed. It would be our last Christmas in our beloved Czech/Slovak land. Early in the month we hosted Elder and Sister Dellenbach from the Area Presidency at our semiannual district conference. Following our meetings, Elder and Sister Dellenbach wanted to see downtown Prague. It was

December 6, Saint Nicholas Day, and much to our delight there was a huge crowd in the city. This was quite a contrast to the near-empty streets when we had arrived two and a half years earlier. People then were put under surveillance if more than two or three gathered together. Now, a Saint Nicholas parade had just disbanded! Children everywhere were dressed in costumes, and colored lights adorned the street. I could not believe it! Where did all those lights come from? I linked my arm through Sister Dellenbach's in excitement, so as not to get separated in the throng. "Look, Sister Dellenbach, the lights are on!" I exclaimed, pointing to the colorfully lighted street. And again I gazed at the lighted shop windows—"The lights are on!" Then again, as I looked upward at the colorful strands sparkling across the street, this time with tears streaming down my face, "The lights are on!"

She smiled at me and softly said, "Of course, Sister Winder, the gospel has come."

> All now rejoice; the long night is o'er.
> Truth is on earth once more!
> Oh, how glorious from the throne above
> Shines the gospel light of truth and love!

BARBARA W. WINDER *served as general president of the Relief Society from April 1984 to April 1990. She is the mother of three sons and one daughter and fifteen grandchildren. In addition to serving with her husband in the Czech/Slovak Mission, she served with him as he presided in the California San Diego Mission from 1982 to 1984. She served as an assistant matron in the Jordan River Temple from 1993 to 1996.*

The Gift of Presence

Art E. Berg

As a young man I was eager to serve a mission. From the time I was eight years old, I counted the days until I could serve the Lord in a full-time capacity. In the years I awaited the official call, I wondered where in all the world the Lord might send me. I had one friend who went to South Africa, another who went to Korea, and still another who served in Japan. I wasn't interested only in foreign missions; there were also many places in the United States where I would have loved to have served. As a boy, I had traveled with my family all over the United States visiting relatives. By the time I was eighteen, I had seen forty-two of the fifty states.

On the day my mission call came, I was as eager as any young man would be. My family gathered around me, and we all held our breaths as I tore the letter from the envelope. I would be a little less than honest if I didn't say that I was somewhat disappointed when I read that I would be spending the next two years of my life in North and South Dakota. After I figured out which country those places were in, I asked my father why, in all of our family travels, we had never been to North or South Dakota. He replied, "Son, when you get there, you'll know!"

My first area was in Mandan, North Dakota. It was a small community beside the Missouri River. While the people were principled and God-fearing, they were not very fond of "outsiders." North Dakotans almost had a sense of pride about their harsh and frigid winters. They felt their winters kept the "riff-raff" out. I felt like I was Elder Riff and my companion was Elder Raff.

My first winter in the Dakotas was one of the coldest on record. I remember one day we tracted for more than three hours in below-zero temperatures—53 degrees below zero! We were so bundled with clothes, coats, scarfs, and gloves that all you could see from beneath our protection was the determination in our eyes. Our feet were frozen and our hands numb, but still no one would let us in, whether to receive our gift of the gospel of Christ or to offer us a cup of hot chocolate. Their hearts seemed to be as cold as their winters.

As Christmas neared, I began to feel pangs of loneliness. I felt like a stranger in a foreign land, among a people who didn't dislike me as much as they just ignored me. I'm not sure which was worse. My heart

Our feet were frozen and our hands numb, but still no one would let us in, whether to receive our gift of the gospel of Christ or to offer us a cup of hot chocolate. Their hearts seemed to be as cold as their winters.

longed for the smells and sights of a familiar Christmas. I yearned to be with family and friends who loved me. I was finding it difficult to keep a gentle tear from rolling down my frozen cheek from time to time.

On Christmas Eve, all of the missionaries in the area gathered together at a member's home for dinner. The smells of turkey and hot homemade rolls emanated from the direction of the kitchen. A soft, crackling fire popped in the corner of the room. Stockings hung from the chimney with children's names on them. Everything looked familiar. But still there was a hollow, empty feeling in my heart. In a room full of people, I felt alone. That's the most terrible kind of loneliness there is.

After dinner, we crowded into the small living room to watch a 16 mm film of a movie I had never heard of or seen before—*It's a Wonderful Life*—with Jimmy Stewart. As we watched, the room began to feel warmer, not in temperature, but in spirit. The movie reminded me that even under the worst of circumstances, there is a lot to be grateful for. My heart filled with gratitude and thanksgiving. The film taught that the measure of a person's life could be found, at least in part, in his relationships with others. Although the principal character of the movie, George Bailey, felt very much alone in his frustration and seemingly hopeless plight, he found comfort in his guardian angel, Clarence, who never left his side. My purpose and vision as a missionary became clearer as I felt the influence of the Spirit whispering to my heart.

Unashamed, I let tears fall from my eyes and I wept as a child.

In the final moments of the classic film, Clarence the angel leaves a book which includes the personal inscription, "No man is a failure who has friends." I wasn't alone anymore. I looked around the room and, perhaps for the first time, saw other missionaries who shared the same heartfelt desires to serve the Lord as I had; only now they weren't just companions, but friends.

But something even more significant happened. I felt the presence of the Lord in a special way. More than just sensing his presence, I felt his love for me. For that moment, my heart felt embraced by the understanding, empathy, and compassion of my Savior. And despite the fact that I was a stranger in a foreign land, I didn't feel alone anymore. I knew from that moment that I had a friend I could trust in forever, a friend who would never leave or fail me. I had received a most wonderful Christmas gift that served me for the remainder of my missionary experience.

Having served the eighteen-month mission that was required at that time, I was home again for my next Christmas with my family in sunny California. I rejoiced in the experiences of my mission—but even then I never realized how significant that Christmas gift from my Savior would become.

After enjoying a traditional California Christmas at home with my family, I prepared to travel to Utah to spend the rest of the holidays with my fiancée and her family. I left on Christmas evening with a friend of mine named John. I drove for the first eight and a half hours, then grew tired and swapped places with John, who drove away into the night. I soon fell asleep in the passenger seat. John drove for the next hour or hour and a half; then he too became tired and fell asleep at the wheel.

The car hit the corner of a concrete divider and rolled down the side of the road a number of times. Despite the fact that I was wearing a seat belt, I was ejected from the vehicle. The car finally came to a stop in a pile of twisted metal and broken glass. John, still in the driver's seat, looked to his right to see if I was okay. I wasn't there!

Lying on the cold desert floor, I could feel the warmth of the blood on my face. My neck and head surged with such intense pain I thought I was going to explode. I struggled to lift myself from the earth, but I couldn't move. It was then that I realized that I couldn't feel my legs and that I couldn't move my hands. I was paralyzed from the chest down.

In the still air of the crisp night, I felt alone. I knew that what had happened was terrible. I knew it was serious. Where had all my dreams gone? I was twenty-one years old. It was the morning after Christmas. A time for celebration? Love? Joy? Family? It was four-thirty in the morning, still dark outside. My future looked as dark as the sky above me. The pain

Lying on the cold desert floor, I could feel the warmth of the blood on my face. My neck and head surged with such intense pain I thought I was going to explode. I struggled to lift myself from the earth, but I couldn't move.

was greater than I could bear, and I could feel myself slipping into unconsciousness. God help me!

It started as a small, warm feeling and quickly grew to an overwhelming surge of confidence. I was not alone! The Lord of the sparrows and lilies had not overlooked his broken and hurting son lying in the desert. In a moment, I knew in my heart that God had not forgotten me. I knew he loved me and, perhaps even more significantly, that he would never stop. In perhaps the darkest hour of my life, I felt the very real presence and love of my Savior. I was not alone and, by his promise, I never will be. Tears stung the open wounds on my face.

Whatever the future would hold for me (and I am paralyzed to this day), I knew it could not include failure. "No man is a failure who has friends." And I had the greatest friend of all—He who descended beneath all things to lift me up. I would never be alone again. For a second time, I had received the greatest gift of all for Christmas—not in the form of presents, but presence. And I thank God for that.

ART E. BERG *is a professional speaker and president of Invictus Communications, Inc. A popular speaker for Brigham Young University's Especially for Youth and Know Your Religion programs, he is also the author of* Some Miracles Take Time *and* Finding Peace in Troubled Waters.

Riding into Light Aboard the American Flyer Train

RICHARD H. CRACROFT

THOUGH I WOULD NOT realize it until a few more Christmases would prove that I had indeed changed my youthful perspective on Christmas gifts, my twelfth Christmas was a turning point in my understanding of my mother and father, and thus of myself and life—and of the profound spiritual meaning to be found even in Christmas presents, proving again the Lord's profound utterance that "all things unto me are spiritual." (D&C 29:34.)

By all things being *spiritual*, I mean, of course, even an American Flyer electric train complete with searchlight car, log-dumper, and freight cars capable of trundling my tiny, homemade aerial bombs from my ship-lined, Lincoln-Log docks at my basement Pearl Harbor to my inverted-shoebox Hickam Field, near the fruit room. There the bombs were loaded by an assortment of tin and plastic soldiers onto two dozen assorted model airplane Spitfires, Hellcats, P-38s, and B-29s (and secured with elastic bands) for dropping atop my assortment of Japanese destroyers and Zero-carrying aircraft carriers, all of which, heady with sneak-attack victory, were eternally steaming towards Midway (etched in black paint on my playroom floor) and decisive engagement with American aircraft launched from the U.S. Pacific Fleet (a motley of carriers and destroyers, as well as submarines and PT boats that were, to the confounding of the literal-minded, larger than the battleships). These valiant soldiers, sailors, and airmen (me, me, and me) would, again and again, successfully annihilate the hapless Japanese forces (played, generously, by me) in wonderfully noisy battles which lasted nearly twenty minutes per engagement. My men and I, accompanied by stirring strains of martial music (trilled and hummed by me), would change the course of history at least three times a week and twice on Saturday in the spacious underground war-room at 1067 East 4th South, Salt Lake City, 2, Utah (tel. 4-4448). The neighbors lived in blissful ignorance of the recurring devastation going on beneath their very noses under a redoubtable youthful commander (me), who combined in his deceptively youthful exterior the best qualities of MacArthur, Marshall, Patton, Nimitz, Eisenhower, Stillwell, Doolittle, Chennault, Ridgeway, Pappy Boyington, and John Wayne.

The key to completing the deployment of Allied and Axis forces for this thrice-weekly Armageddon was a much-needed, sturdy freight train—for transportation of matériel from the docks at Pearl to the fighters and bombers at Hickam Field, some ten feet downwind—capable of withstanding repeated bombings from unrelenting Japanese Zeros and Mitsubishis. I had longed for this train for at least two Christmases, as a functioning replacement for the sad-looking, three-rail model train that had belonged to my brother Paul back when naive kids were still excited about Lindbergh's flight, before the dawning of glorious modern warfare. I had long before set up Paul's battered, useless old train as a kind of target train, like the USS *Utah*, and repeatedly blew it off its tracks with well-placed, screaming dive-bombings. I needed that new train if I was to recover from the December 7 attack and get on with winning the war in the Pacific.

Yet now, moving about the living room straightening up after the last of the Thanksgiving guests had departed, I began to understand what Mom, with strained and haggard face, was struggling to tell me: This year the war effort would have to get on without the train; I would not be getting *anything* for Christmas, much less a $12 American Flyer freight train complete with searchlight and log-unloader (read: bomb-unloader) and troop and bomb transport cars.

Like a bomber pilot who has just realized that his thirty-seconds-over-Tokyo would end in a forced landing far short of Guam, I began to realize that Dad's recent blindness was beginning to threaten the

I began to understand what Mom, with strained and haggard face, was struggling to tell me: I would not be getting anything for Christmas, much less a $12 American Flyer freight train complete with searchlight and log-unloader.

self-centered neatness and security of my twelve-year-old world. With guests departed, Dad had retired to one of few pleasures in his newly darkened existence: the Talking Book in the back room. There, instead of recreating the attack on Pearl Harbor, he would listen on 33 1/3 rpm recordings to another of Captain Horn-blower's adventures.

I would never forget Dad's first hesitating steps down that DC-3 rollstep earlier that November, or the disturbing despair on the faces of my mother, sister, and aunts as their eyes followed Dad with his dark glasses, hospital pallor, and tight features. His nearly three-month hospital stay in Evanston, Illinois—for his fourth eye surgery in as many years—had finally plunged him from the heights of successful cataract surgeries and 20/20 vision to, first, a failed detached-retina surgery and blindness in his left eye; and then, a year later, to his present darkness, unenlightened by the best efforts of world-renowned surgeons to reattach his right retina. Ralph Cracroft, age fifty, came home to us permanently blind, and he would spend the rest of his life learning and understanding the remarkable spiritual blessing this new state would be for him and all of his family. But that's another story.

"You see, Dick," Mom was saying, fluffing up the sofa pillows, "we simply won't have much of a Christmas this year. I mean, you know, no train . . . nothing." She said this with a sigh and groan that rose from somewhere between her toes. She knew how hard

Ralph Cracroft, age fifty, came home to us permanently blind, and he would spend the rest of his life learning and understanding the remarkable spiritual blessing this new state would be for him and all of his family.

I labored, each year, to lighten Santa Claus's load at my address. I had been, for six or seven years past, the inveterate and inexhaustible catalog-searcher and solemn recorder of lists of Christmas presents. Lying on my stomach before the Atwood-Kent radio and listening to "Inner Sanctum Mystery," "Mr. District Attorney," "It Pays to Be Ignorant," "Jack Benny," and "Fibber McGee and Molly," I made lists of presents—for me, of course—carefully labeled, "Must Have," "Should Have," "Could Use," "Possible," and "Next Year," and went to bed on Christmas Eve with loudly voiced statements of faith in God, in Church, and in Santa, knowing they were all Equally True—and no doubt causing my parents to tremble before the inevitability of my disappointment the following morning. Mother also knew, however, that somehow I was never disappointed, ever resilient, and always happily satisfied with Santa's Choice, even if he never got past the first two or three items on my interminable lists, which had all been mailed at the post office, my father assured me, and then promptly forgotten by me. Still, Mom knew what destruction her words were to my hopes: this year I had set aside all lists and declared for the American Flyer train—nothing else.

Motioning me to sit down on the doily-backed chair, Mother laid it all out with an earnestness I had seen only on Great Occasions. So I listened carefully, and as I listened it all suddenly dawned on me. And, though I did not know it then, I crossed a bridge out of childhood and watched my American Flyer train drop off that same bridge into a bottomless abyss. I finally understood what had been in the air around our house for several weeks: Nothing would ever be the same again. My $5,000-a-year accountant father had no job; and though he would shortly begin a rehabilitation course at the Murray B. Allen Center for the Blind, he would not become a wage-earner again for many months; in the meantime he would be making brooms and rubber doormats. My mother, who had not had a job since her marriage in 1918, had already begun a tiring (and humbling) routine of cleaning other people's houses and caring for infirm and dying old men and women. (She would soon find happy and lifelong employment in the Office of the Presiding Bishop, but we didn't know it then.) And I, the only child still at home, had already begun a job—arranged for by a thoughtful principal and caring teachers—as a student custodian at Roosevelt Jr. High at $18 per month. Now Mother talked to me of mortgage payments, utility bills, and the cost of groceries—and of the necessity of my putting my wages, after tithing, into the family till.

I agreed at once, pleased to be asked to contribute. Suddenly I was staring adulthood in the face. And amidst the stare I saw a father privately weeping as he attempted to learn Braille ("I'm feeling *badly* today," he would chuckle grammatically, rubbing his desensitized fingers); as he walked into doors carelessly left half-opened; as he stumbled off curbs while learning to walk to and from church with a long white cane; as he cut and gouged and roughed his hands while making rubber mats; as he polished his tan shoes with black polish; as he, thinking himself alone, sobbed aloud, "O God, where art thou?" to an ever-darkened room.

And I saw my mother emerge from their bedroom with swollen eyes to greet us all with a sheepish smile, and, wiping away her tears, ask Dad to read aloud to her from his Braille Book of Mormon; I saw her learn, then instruct me, how to tell Dad at dinnertime that the peas on his plate were at two o'clock, the cut-up pork chop at six, and the potatoes at nine; and I watched her, weary from a day at work, join him at dishwashing and drying—now his task—for their regular and truly lovely duet rendering of "An Angel from on High." And somehow I found myself doing the house-cleaning, scrubbing the floors, ironing my own clothes, landscaping the yard, and doing home repairs—all the while undertaking to destroy the Japanese fleet at Midway, *without* an American Flyer train.

Gradually, imperceptibly, I began to sense that the real drama going on in the Cracroft household late that fall, as that first post-blindness Christmas approached, was not *my* tragic loss of *my* American Flyer train, but the daily triumphs of a good man and a good woman who had been whiplashed off course by circumstance and were bound and determined to put

And I saw my mother emerge from their bedroom with swollen eyes to greet us all with a sheepish smile, and, wiping away her tears, ask Dad to read aloud to her from his Braille Book of Mormon.

on a neckbrace, paste on a smile, and get back on track. Reflecting back, it is clear that I was beginning to accept and even enjoy the bit part I was playing in this real-life drama.

When Christmas morning dawned and brothers and sister and their spouses filed, as we always did, hand-on-shoulder into the living room singing "We wish you a merry Christmas," I was fully prepared for the inevitable: There, partially set up in front of the Christmas tree, was Paul's old electric train, minus the engine. As I knelt down before the train, pasty smile on my face and lump of lead in my throat, Mom said, in her cheeriest, "We have taken the engine in to be repaired, Dick, but he had to order parts and couldn't get it finished until after New Year's."

"That's great," I lied, registering that my sister, Helen, was looking at me with veiled pity. "Hey, I wasn't expecting anything; I'll have fun with this train. They don't build 'em like this anymore"—at least *that* was the truth!

"Do you really think this is a great train?" asked my brother Paul.

"Sure," I grinned and nobly began to motion the others to their gifts—after all, they all seemed to have more than I.

"Then maybe you'll let me alone while I play with this one," he chuckled, pulling out a large, flat box from behind the couch, a box boldly proclaiming "American Flyer" on its cover. It was my American Flyer train, with smoking engine, electric switch, searchlight, bomb-unloader, freight-car troop transports, tunnels, station house, and terrain! The whole dream, and more.

I shouted for joy, looked up at Mom with a "How did you do it?" query on my face, and, receiving her "It's all right, son" look in return, I went to work reconstructing Hickam Field and Pearl Harbor on the living room floor, impeded only by my three literal-minded, unimaginative brothers and brother-in-law, lately a Marine Corps Lt. Colonel, Army Lieutenant, and Air Force B-29 pilot, whose inability to balance five-inch bombs atop three-inch planes caused me to wonder how we ever won victory in the Pacific.

Throughout that memorable day, I kept glimpsing amidst my joys a hand-holding, beaming mother and father. And, more than that, I glimpsed, for the first time since that fall, *hope*. And in my confusion and happiness, I saw that hope was somehow emblemized for us all in that American Flyer train; and that, after all, "all things unto [the Lord and me] are spiritual." After a dark night at our house, morning had somehow gotten turned on again; life would go on; things suddenly looked bright for all of us once more.

And it turned out to be so. The tide had turned. But only for some, for the advent of that American Flyer meant the repeated demise of my hapless Japanese fleet—and, for me, again and again, week upon week, the (well-deserved) Congressional Medal of Honor.

Throughout that memorable day, I kept glimpsing amidst my joys a hand-holding, beaming mother and father. And, more than that, I glimpsed, for the first time since that fall, hope.

RICHARD H. CRACROFT *is professor of English at Brigham Young University, where he has also generaled as department chair and dean of the College of Humanities. He and his wife, Janice Alger Cracroft, have three children who learned to reenact Pearl Harbor in a number of sandpiles, where their father joined them amidst a variety of campaigns as bishop, stake president, and mission president (Zurich, Switzerland). He is now training grandchildren in the fine art of make-believe war in the Pacific.*

Christmas Is Christmas Wherever You Are

Wm. Grant Bangerter

Both before and after I was called as a General Authority of the Church, I was sometimes assigned to live and work in foreign countries. At first, my wife and I wondered how our children would do in new and strange situations. We wondered how we would feel without our home. We soon found that no matter where we went, when we were in the service of the Lord we were *not* strangers or foreigners but were fellow-citizens in the household of God—and *we were "Home."*

In April 1974, President Kimball was presiding over his first general conference as the prophet. He announced his intent to open the gospel in areas and countries where we had not previously been able to send missionaries. As the Saints prayed for the doors of the nations to open, the Lord responded almost immediately by unlocking the doors of Portugal. I was called to establish the mission, and I was given four missionaries to begin the work. We arrived in Lisbon just before Thanksgiving. In our group were my wife, five of our children, and the four missionaries. As the Christmas season descended upon us, we became involved in setting up our home in an unfamiliar place and adjusting to the business and legal arrangements of opening a new mission and country.

One of the first orders of business was to establish our living arrangements. We got busy looking for furniture. We had begun by sleeping on mattresses on the floor, but rather than buying expensive bedsteads, I put my carpenter expertise to work and enlisted the help of my family to build box-bases out of plywood for our mattresses. My wife made a matching skirt for each of their bedspreads.

With the missionaries, our family now numbered eleven. Another member family—the Ray Caldwells from Canada, who were serving in the Canadian embassy (he was First Secretary there)—had been holding meetings in their home, which was near to ours. Almost immediately, an employee of the U.S. embassy, Steve Lindsey, found us; and two young U.S. navy personnel surfaced from the NATO offices: John Peterson and Marilyn Dalton.

The climate, while cool, was similar to northern California's with its almost-constant rainy weather. We did our shopping under umbrellas with sloshing water underfoot. In this new land there was no snow, there were no Christmas trees, there wasn't much of anything

We did our shopping under umbrellas with sloshing water underfoot. In this new land there was no snow, there were no Christmas trees, there wasn't much of anything to embellish the home with Christmas adornments.

to embellish the home with Christmas adornments. The nation of Portugal had been limited in its progress under a dictatorship of restraint for fifty years. The revolution that had inadvertently opened the doors to the gospel had removed the political restraints, but there was not much in the economy to excite the Spirit of Christmas. There were no sparkling lights and a very limited number of items for purchase in the shops— although people in this Christian nation emphasized and celebrated the traditions of Christmas in their own unique and enjoyable way.

Our children, aged from seventeen down to nine, embarked on the new experience with no regrets; but as parents, my wife and I wondered how we could make this season a time of celebration and excitement for them. Our new house was bare, the living arrangements were foreign and strange, and we needed something to bring life to the season.

Two days before Christmas we decided that we desperately needed a piano. Our sixteen-year-old daughter, Peggy, played well, and we wanted to sing songs of the season, as well as what we called our "homesick" songs (such as "O Home Beloved Where E'er I Wander" and "Springtime in the Rockies") and some of those special songs we had learned in Brazil, which we could sing to our missionaries and the Portuguese neighbors. These included "Papai Noel" (Santa Claus) and "Noite Feliz" (Silent Night).

We began our search. Pianos did not seem to

exist in the stores, but finally we located one place downtown in Lisbon that had a used upright piano. We arranged the purchase and asked when it could be delivered. The manager said, "Maybe tomorrow." Sister Bangerter responded, "No, we must have it delivered this evening." It was already late in the afternoon, but with this insistence the man agreed. We rejoiced. We were finally ready for the holiday. What a happy surprise, a perfect delight for the whole family! It was all we would need in gifts for Christmas.

Our four missionaries came back to the mission home to spend Christmas Eve, staying the night. Two were native Brazilians and two were from the United States. We planned a happy supper to bring them into a feeling of comfort and something like a home. We arranged bedding on the floor to give the elders a place to sleep. The Caldwells also joined us for the evening.

After the meal, members of our family went to their dresser drawers, and the elders went to their backpacks, and we each pulled out a sock to hang on a clothesline we'd set up in the living room. It was a homely and laughable sight Santa would find for his limited offering.

As the evening progressed, three or four young Portuguese boys, each about fifteen years of age, came knocking on the door. One had an old ukulele with two strings missing. We invited them in and listened as they tried to sing a little ditty ("Boas Festas, Boas Festas") while he strummed on the strings. After their song they waited for us to give them money, which we did, along with an offering of something to eat.

That visit reminded us of the caroling we had traditionally done for our neighbors back in Utah, and we suddenly felt the missionary urge to call on and sing to some of our new neighbors! With our family, the missionaries, and the Caldwell family, we visited several of the houses nearby.

We soon discovered that it was a challenge to convince our neighbors to open their homes to us; they assumed that we were another group of caroling boys from town, looking for a tip or a handout. We persisted, however, and they were delighted to discover that we were their neighbors from down or across the street, simply making a call to wish them the Spirit of Christmas.

One neighbor was an official of the Brazilian embassy. As our group entered that home, the family listened to our singing of songs from their homeland that they had not heard for ten years. Tears of longing welled up in their eyes. Across the street was the home of a businessman from Germany. We will never forget the dignity and reverence they displayed—the father, mother, and their young son, all dressed formally for Christmas Eve at home. They seemed very lonesome in their quiet setting, wanting to find something to touch their feelings of home. They wept as we harmonized the three verses of "Silent Night." In return, they sang "Silent Night" to us in German, then expressed

They seemed very lonesome, wanting to find something to touch their feelings of home. They wept as we harmonized the three verses of "Silent Night." In return, they sang "Silent Night" to us in German.

appreciation for our offerings of warmth and friendship on Christmas Eve. Somehow, our own hearts and eyes seemed to glow and burn as the Spirit of Christmas stamped an unforgettable impression on our souls.

This never-to-be-forgotten Christmas was much like we'd have had at home, though of course it was modified because of our circumstances. The gifts were surprisingly plentiful. There was a continued celebration of games (including outdoor games on the beach), singing in Portuguese, and visiting and spending time with the elders and the Caldwell family. Throughout the day, we each stored up the inward spiritual force needed to launch us in the pioneering effort of opening a new country to the gospel and beginning our missionary labors in the days and months to come. Though we were thousands of miles from "home," the Lord had us in his palm, touched us, and through us, touched others. We felt that no matter where we happened to live, while we were in his service we always would be "home."

ELDER WM. GRANT BANGERTER *was called to be an Assistant to the Quorum of the Twelve Apostles in 1975 (while still in Portugal) and a member of the First Quorum of the Seventy a year later. He served in the presidency of the First Quorum of the Seventy from September 1978 to April 1980 and from February 1985 to October 1989. For nearly ten years, he was executive director of the Church's temple department, from 1980 until October 1989, when he was given emeritus status as a General Authority.*

Barney—
or the Bishop's Son?

KRIS MACKAY

MY MOST MEMORABLE CHRISTMAS? No contest! But unusual as it may sound to you who are unfamiliar with the story, that particular silent night, that holy night—the night that altered my destiny forever—took place years before I was even born. Let me explain.

Katie Marie Dana stood before the bedroom mirror one December evening in her parents' Ogden, Utah, home. Slowly brushing her beautiful, naturally curly, honey-red hair, preparing herself for bed, she paused, deep in thought. Which should it be? Not that she needed to make a decision right away. She was only sixteen, after all. For months now, she and two wonderful young men had been as companionable as The Three Musketeers. Katie hadn't known who she was actually "going with," and up to that night she hadn't cared. When one came to her home, they both came. The trio went everywhere together, not as literal dates, but gravitating together instantly whenever and wherever their paths happened to cross. Like tonight's Christmas sleigh ride, for instance.

Ward leaders had organized the outing for the youth. Katie was the last on the list to be picked up and, quick as a flash, Barney, the newcomer from Norway, and Ray Terry, the bishop's son, scooted apart and made room for her to squeeze in between them. She wasn't surprised. By then a pattern had definitely developed.

Their conveyance was packed. They snuggled in with other happy teenagers on the floor of a wagon bed, sitting on nice, clean straw with plenty of warm blankets to keep out the cold. In preparation, the wagon's wheels had been replaced by runners, putting them close to the ground. It was such fun gliding smoothly and silently over the snow, hearing the jingle of sleigh bells attached to the harnesses of two powerful horses pulling the sleigh, and watching puffs of "smoke" billow from the animals' nostrils, from their exertion in the crisp night air. It was a night filled with magic.

But all things must end, even magical sleigh rides. Back home again, holding the brush momentarily suspended above her head, she wondered for the first time. This arrangement—like the sleigh ride—couldn't go on forever. Who should she eventually choose? They were both so *nice*. Each had his good points. Ray was taller. He was dark and he was definitely handsome, with the added distinction of being the bishop's son. The brush stroked her hair one more time while she pondered.

On the other hand, Barney was quiet. But he was steady, levelheaded, mature, and reliable in all things. And he also was good-looking, though in a less flamboyant way.

She wasn't consciously attempting to decide then and there, but she remembers leaning noticeably toward Ray. He was more outgoing, more flashy, somehow more exciting to a young girl's imagination. Laying her brush aside and pulling her flannel nightgown over her head, then slipping between the cold sheets of the bed, her subconscious must have been more involved than she suspected, because that night she had a dream so vivid that every detail was as clear to her sixty years later as if it were happening again for the very first time.

In the dream, Katie found herself standing all alone on the back porch. The night was crystal clear. She looked up to see the dark sky laden with brilliant, twinkling stars. Gradually she became aware that she was praying with all the fervor and anxiety of which she was capable, pleading to know which of the two was right for her. In her dream state, she realized that decision was the most momentous she would ever be called upon to make.

Suddenly every star in the sky began falling, swirling, up, down, and around in a dizzying dance. The girl was terrified. Was the world coming to an end before she'd had time to really live?

She watched, horrified, for perhaps a minute, maybe two, barely able to breathe, until the stars

In the dream, Katie found herself standing all alone on the back porch. She looked up to see the dark sky laden with brilliant, twinkling stars. Gradually she became aware that she was praying with all the fervor and anxiety of which she was capable.

ceased their wild, uncoordinated flurry and began to take shape. At last they came together in a long dazzling strip stretching from one side of the heavens to the other, and when they were finally at rest, their light spelled out the name

BARNEY KRISTOFFERSON

Katie has never considered that to be an ordinary dream, but felt it was the advice or will of the Lord. Ray soon dropped out of the race. His mother confided that she had been a little disturbed at this unusual pattern of dating and had told Ray he should either cut Barney out of the threesome or bow out himself. So, sympathetic to the depth of his friend's feelings, he graciously did the latter.

Katie and Barney—my mother and father—saw more and more of each other for the next three years and, in the process, fell deeper and deeper in love. Their first official date was on January 11. They celebrated that anniversary each year thereafter as even more important than the day of their marriage three years later, which was on January 16.

Each week during the winter months they went to Pantage's vaudeville theater to enjoy a play, and stopped afterwards at a favorite restaurant for a snack. In the summertime, they went to Hot Springs for a swim. Sometimes they rode the streetcar up Ogden Canyon to the Hermitage, an amusement park where Wheeler and Ogden canyons branch off from one another. But their favorite outing of all was to Lagoon, another amusement park reached by taking the Bamberger train to a little town called Kaysville. The train stopped conveniently at Lagoon's front gate.

One unforgettable date was scheduled for what turned out to be the coldest, most blustery night of the year. Deep snow covered the ground knee-high, and a strong wind blew the falling snowflakes about, making it impossible to see more than a few feet ahead. And, in those days, Barney didn't have access to a telephone.

Katie, worried for his safety, kept vigil at the window, straining to see him approaching up the street. Her mother said over and over, "Katie, you might as well stop looking. He won't come out on a night like this." But Katie knew him. She knew he would come. He was late, but finally there he was, bent double, almost losing his struggle against the force of the wind. He was late because he had crossed a pasture near his home and twice became disoriented, not able to see where he was going. But he never gave up. His dependability that night was a precursor to their married life.

Theirs was the proverbial marriage made in heaven. As a young wife, Katie worried again when it seemed they might not be able to conceive, but finally, over time, they became the parents of six children (four girls, a boy, and another girl—and I was the third girl of the bunch). They are the grandparents of twenty and great-grandparents of many others—I'm afraid I've lost count. Growing up in their home was a happy time.

Her mother said over and over, "Katie, you might as well stop looking. He won't come out on a night like this." But Katie knew he would come. Finally there he was, bent double, almost losing his struggle against the force of the wind.

None of us recalls hearing an argument or an angry word ever spoken between them.

I don't personally remember this, my most memorable Christmas, but I have no doubt that my brother and sisters and I were deeply involved. No doubt we were peeking down between the swirling stars while our futures were being decided that awesome night, and I also have no doubt that we might have nudged an errant star or two in their journey across the sky to form our father's name.

Our beloved Dad was called back to heaven four years ago, passing peacefully in the night, and by now Mother's memory for details isn't what it once was. I can't ask her for the exact date and be sure. I'm not certain that the night the Lord took a hand in the destiny of all their descendants was Christmas Eve on the dot, but I like to think it *was* Christmas Eve when every star in the heavens moved. At the very least, I know it was during that glorious, sacred season—a season to celebrate not only the miraculous and holy birth of our Savior, Heavenly Father's Only Begotten Son, but also the miraculous birth of our family.

KRIS MACKAY *is a freelance writer from Fair Oaks, California. She is the author of five books, including* No Greater Love, *and coauthor of* The Confident You. *She has also been published in* Reader's Digest *and* Parade.

Three Wise Gifts

Elaine Cannon

Soft is the sound of Christmas. *Soft* has other definitions but it speaks of Christmas to me.

Soft songs. Carols heard through muting snowflakes. "Silent Night," a sacramental hymn the meeting before Christmas. Primary children cooing "Jesus Once Was a Little Child." Toddlers caught up, and believing, tirelessly humming lullabies to the Baby Jesus in the family crèche. "O Little Town of Bethlehem" on the car radio—cozy-calm in a traffic jam.

Soft lights—votive candles, ebbing coals on the hearth, tiny twinkles on the tree, flashlight in Santa's attic or on garage rafters.

Soft answers turning away unwanted wrath from stressful preparations for joy.

Soft whispering, shared secrets, sweet murmuring beneath the mistletoe. Soft touch, new emotion, deeper, finer.

Soft embraces friend for friend, for relatives coming home, for neighbors bearing tasty offerings, as part of the "Behold your little ones" goodnight ritual.

Soft, so soft, the skin of an infant.

Soft, calming, too, when Luke 2 is read aloud last thing Christmas Eve.

Soft memories of Christmases past, and with it all, the softening of the heart with gifts that mean more than money can buy. Over the years I have received three wise gifts, wrapped with subtle undertones, that prolong the season of softness forever. The first gift is *thoughtfulness*. The second gift is *understanding*. The third gift is the *tender hurt of happiness*. Each in its way adds nuances to old themes, depth to traditions, and healing to the heart.

THE FIRST WISE GIFT: THOUGHTFULNESS

Toy soldiers, Christmas nutcrackers, and the Royal Guard of Britain had nothing on the six-year-old in wire-frame glasses with a shock of straw hair standing steel-spine straight at my opened door. He held a gift of goodies high against his shoulder like a firearm, but he didn't turn over the basket at once, for he knew the correct order of things—there was caroling to be done first. With a nod of his head signaling the back-up chorus, he led the group in belting out "God Rest Ye Merry Gentlemen." Their teacher stood smiling in the background.

It was not a *soft* sound of Christmas; it was the jubilant cry of show-offs celebrating. A couple of measures into the song the boy stopped short, waving his free arm and ordering, "No! No! Stop!"

Somebody groaned, "Bradley James, you've ruined the whole thing."

"I have not ruined the whole thing. It is the wrong song."

"It's the same song we've always sung first!" Sarah Beesley explained with exaggerated patience.

"Well, it is the wrong song. We should have thought about it. This isn't a gentleman at the door. This is a grandma. How can we sing 'God Rest Ye Merry Gentlemen' to a grandma? You have just ruined Christmas," he pronounced formally.

"Bradley James, you can *not* ruin Christmas. No way!" Little Sarah Beesley, twig from pioneer roots (and musical genius), was irate.

I saved the moment by ushering the carolers inside; Bradley James pointed where each should sit before he marched mechanically to center stage in front of the fireplace. With a smart turn, he positioned himself rigidly in the role of master of ceremonies—six going on forty-five; innocent but recognizing the essential of rising to the occasion.

Bradley James lowered the Christmas gift basket from his shoulder to the hearth and straddled it with stiff legs, an action that revealed an unzipped fly in his new Christmas slacks.

Valiantly ignoring the giggles and nudges, Bradley James muttered "Oops!" as he spun around to

"Well, it is the wrong song. We should have thought about it. This isn't a gentleman at the door. This is a grandma. How can we sing 'God Rest Ye Merry Gentlemen' to a grandma?"

close the offending zipper. Spiffy now, he whirled back around, thumbed each red suspender while announcing the program slowly, softly, reverently. That is to say, he licked his lips, puffed his cheeks, smacked his tongue against the blank space in the top row of his teeth, sighed under the weight of mishaps and self-importance, as well as the rigors of suppressing his lively personality.

The Sunday School singers moved easily through traditional tunes, chose a chocolate from the tray at hand, and then, in a mood of worship, they caroled "Silent Night" while filing toward the front door.

"Wait! Wait!" Bradley James was frantic. "The Christmas basket!" He wanted an audience to see his presentation because his basket was *different* from the others they had given. He had thought things over and, according to the teacher whispering in my ear, he had taken a special interest in filling it.

"This basket has candy, fruit, and nuts down here," he said, stirring up the contents. "But this is the best part—I put in a can of chicken noodle soup because it is good for you!"

"This basket has candy, fruit, and nuts down here," he said, stirring up the contents. "But this is the best part—I put in a can of chicken noodle soup because it is good for you!" This last part with a stage whisper and knowing glance. Then he called out, "Merry Christmas! And don't forget the soup!" I never have.

Bradley James had thrust the basket toward me flashing a smile of soft sunshine into a wintry life. It was the wonderful wise Gift of Thoughtfulness.

THE SECOND WISE GIFT: UNDERSTANDING

Dreams don't always come true, even at

Christmas. Sometimes, life being what it is, the proverbial biggest gift under the tree is for someone else. Sometimes there is no gift. Sometimes Santa and Jesus get equal timing. Now and then an experience underscores that glorious event of *Christmas,* softening the season to its rightful proportions.

For example, one year the Christmas program in our church included a speaker who was financially successful and a family man, a talented and a socially confident high priest. Mark Rose stood at the pulpit with moist eyes as he delivered a sermon that became my everlasting second wise gift—understanding.

Mark-who-had-everything told the unforgettable story from his childhood that annually had brought forth the cry, "Tell me again, Daddy. Tell me again about your best Christmas."

When Mark's father, Paul, was a little boy, he lived in a small community a great distance from a town or a store, and could not harbor traditions like lavish family-filled stockings. There was no hope of Santa himself finding their town, and there was no such thing as a Sub-for-Santa program.

But there was the annual Christmas social.

Every child counted the days until the Christmas social. The traditional program and refreshment were crowned with The Gift for each child's Christmas (furnished by the parents.)

One year, things went awry. Just before the event, Paul's big brother Horace was hurried to Salt

Lake for an appendectomy and his mother went with him. The father was bishop, and in the circumstance of timing, trauma, and responsibility for the Christmas social, a gift for Paul was forgotten. Bishop Rose was destitute of anything to offer. Finally, a little red box of raisins taken from his own pocket saved the day.

As the father and son walked through the snow from the little chapel to their home up the hill, Bishop Rose held the boy's small hand tightly every step of the way. Paul told how he remembered his father's fingers squeezing and releasing his little hand all the way home. He remembered, as well, that tears streamed down his father's face, and that his voice sounded funny! The sensitive father explained why there was nothing more for Paul beneath the Christmas tree at the meetinghouse than the red box of raisins. The father's sadness was coupled with a deep desire to never disappoint the boy in any way—particularly at Christmas.

It was a walk of love, an exchange of emotion and closeness such as Paul never had experienced before. Suddenly he *understood*. His father really loved him—loved him in a way he had not imagined!

As the boy grew into the man, he came to understand a father's love for a son, and the depth of love Heavenly Father and his Son Jesus feel for all mortals. New insight came as well, regarding the scripture that says, "silver and gold have I none; but such as I have give I thee." (Acts 3:6.)

Understanding is indeed a wise gift to receive.

THE THIRD WISE GIFT:
THE TENDER HURT OF HAPPINESS

The Nativity never was presented with more significance for me than the day a young friend of mine brought her "special needs class" to our home for a Christmas program. There was a heartbreaking mix of Down's Syndrome and stricken spastics. An unusually abundant spirit accompanied them, as if angels ushered them in.

They were costumed in familiar makeshift robes charmingly depicting the characters. There were Joseph, Mary, and a Herald Angel with a tinsel halo, robed in a twin-size sheet shrouding a wheelchair. There was a shepherd draped in a paisley beach towel with a curved staff carved from styrofoam, mounted on one crutch. A pair of lambs (one on all fours and one wearing a head cage and reclining in a custom-sized canvas stroller) were draped with sheepskin. A small soul held a dowel with a shaking foil star. The Three Wise Men sparkled in recycled and revamped Deseret Industries gowns of lamé, sequins, and velvet.

Make-up surely heightened the drama of things by bolstering confidence in performing. Every one of the participants wore lipstick and rouged cheeks that could neither disguise nor enhance the radiance from a choice eternal spirit within.

The teacher narrated while the needful action was accomplished. There was only one slight change in the script. It was the angel who "brought forth" from the

There were Joseph, Mary, and a Herald Angel with a tinsel halo, robed in a twin-size sheet shrouding a wheelchair. There was a shepherd draped in a paisley beach towel, mounted on one crutch.

side of the wheelchair a swaddled teddy bear ("Firstborn Son") and laid it in *armless* Mary's lap.

By the time the Three Wise Men were propelled onto the scene to nod, bow with clasped hands, or kneel as their afflictions permitted, my soft heart was swollen to the season of wonder! The symbolic gold, frankincense, and myrrh dutifully dumped on the quaint scene became *my* gift—the Tender Hurt of Happiness. The bitter and the incredibly sweet. No one need be exempted from reenacting the gentle, magic Occasion as long as his or her *spirit* was in tune.

This group of Heavenly Father's specially beloved children had gifted me with a dimension that my many seasons had seldom equaled—even when I was hospitalized on the eve of celebration with a threat to my teenage life or when I went into labor for my own baby born at Christmas.

Oh, soft are the sounds of Christmas, and lifting are the wise gifts of the season.

ELAINE CANNON *has been a lecturer for Church Education System programs. She has been a daily columnist for the* Deseret News, *associate editor of the Era of Youth section in the* Improvement Era *and of the* New Era, *and a reporter for such national publications as* Seventeen *and* Better Homes and Gardens. *She is the author of numerous bestselling books. She is a past general president of the Young Women and of Lambda Delta Sigma.*

Christmas in New Guinea

ROBERT L. BACKMAN

M Y MOST MEMORABLE Christmas occurred during World War II in an unlikely setting—Hollandia, New Guinea. To help you understand what happened, let me set the stage.

Some time before that December, I had returned from the mission field and found employment in an electronic tube factory, where my wife and I worked on rotating shifts. Finally World War II caught up with me. I was drafted into the army of the United States and shipped to Texas for basic training in the infantry. I left my wife, pregnant, at home. Those seventeen weeks of training were very difficult, particularly because the environment was extremely foreign to a returned missionary. Thanks to the companionship of other returned missionaries, I survived basic training. Then I held my breath, wondering where I would be assigned.

At that time, the war was raging in Europe, so

many of my fellow trainees were assigned to the European theater. I was surprised to learn that I was headed for the Pacific.

We all received a ten-day "delay en route" before reporting to our embarkation station. I came home to find my wife very large with child, expecting our baby to be born within three weeks. As my ten-day respite came to a close, I hoped I could gain an extension of my leave so I would be present for the birth of our child. With the help of the Red Cross I sent a telegram to the commander of my next station, Fort Ord, requesting an extension. He replied by collect telegram, telling me in no uncertain terms that there was a war on and they desired my immediate presence. I complied, leaving my wife in tears, knowing she would have to deliver our baby without my physical and emotional support.

I reported to Fort Ord feeling I had been cheated out of one of life's great experiences. I was despondent and very unhappy. We immediately started intensive training for combat, my weapons being the heavy mortar and machine guns. Our trainers, all returned veterans from jungle combat, didn't give us much comfort as they told us what to expect in facing the enemy. Their words made me feel even more despondent. I could not perceive of my being in a position where I would be forced to take human life and risk my own.

The day before we shipped overseas, I received a telegram at mail call informing me that my wife had delivered a healthy baby girl. The good news lifted my spirit in one sense, but lowered it as I began to wonder whether I would ever see my sweet daughter—or ever again in this life see my eternal sweetheart. This was to be the last word I had from home for four months.

I shall never forget how I felt as the troop ship steamed out of the San Francisco Bay. I stood on the fantail of the ship watching the Golden Gate—then the shoreline of my country—fade in the distance. I cried bitter tears as we commenced the long voyage across the vast Pacific.

During our voyage, we had to take evasive action to protect ourselves from submarines. We sailed under a complete blackout at night. It was frightening to a young soldier so far from the security of his loved ones and his home. I began to realize that I was headed for war—and that there was a good possibility I would never see my home or family again. I kept thinking to myself that the army would certainly give us more training before we were thrown into combat. It was wishful thinking, a cover for the fear I felt as we drew closer to the war zone.

Twenty-nine days after leaving the shores of America, we finally dropped anchor in Hollandia, New Guinea. It had been such a long, boring trip that we were all happy finally to step ashore, even if we were facing the enemy. Anything seemed better than the cramped quarters, the tasteless food, and the boredom of having nothing to do aboard the troop ship.

The day before we shipped overseas, I received a telegram informing me that my wife had delivered a healthy baby girl. I began to wonder whether I would ever see my sweet daughter—or ever again in this life see my eternal sweetheart.

By the time we landed, Hollandia had been secured. The bay had become a great supply base for the Pacific war zone. Being replacements, we were marched to a tent city to await our assignments to particular combat units.

The weather was so hot and humid it was very uncomfortable. It rained every day, tropical storms that were like cloudbursts back home. We had to ditch our tents with trenches two or three feet deep to handle the runoff. The climate was so damp that we had to build platforms on which to place our boots or they would be rotted overnight. All of our belongings had to be kept off the ground if we wanted to preserve them. We slept under mosquito netting to protect us from the ubiquitous insect population.

While waiting for our assignments, the replacement troops were treated like expendable supplies. To keep us busy, our leaders formed us into labor squads to clear jungle, build defenses, fell trees, and haul supplies from the ships in the bay to the storage tents ashore. It was hard, dirty, exhausting work in that terrible humidity. And it did nothing to make me feel any better about my situation. I wanted to go home.

As Christmas approached we all hoped for a mail call, but we hoped in vain. I kept wondering what my little daughter looked like, how my wife was coping in my absence. I didn't even know what name had been given to my little girl. It was most discouraging.

One day we were detailed to clear some trees.

We entered a grove of magnificent mahogany trees and were handed axes to fell them. As I struck that hard wood with my first blow, the recoil made my arms quiver—while I hardly made a dent in the tree. Since our work was really a project to keep us occupied, no one seemed to care that we did not have the right equipment for the job or made little progress. I stood in awe of those majestic trees that resisted so steadfastly all our feeble efforts to fell them.

Then it was Christmas Day!

I know I was not the only G.I. who hoped our officers would surprise us with a mail call with packages from home. As the day progressed, however, we realized that this was just another day of waiting and working. No mail, no packages, no remembrances from home, no Christmas tree, no lights or ornaments. Nothing! We were granted a few hours of leisure in recognition of the holiday, but that made it even worse. I sat on my cot and thought of home, of my lovely wife and family. I felt bitter that I had been forced to leave all that I held dear to be sitting, uselessly waiting, in a dank, humid jungle on the other side of the world. I wondered what my family would be doing, what Santa Claus had brought them—whether they even thought of lonesome me. Had I been completely forgotten? After all, there was no mail, no Christmas remembrances—not even a card.

I choked back the tears and swallowed the sobs that racked my body. To hide my feelings from my tent

As Christmas Day progressed, we realized that this was just another day of waiting and working. No mail, no packages, no remembrances from home, no Christmas tree, no lights or ornaments. Nothing!

mates, I took a walk, hoping to find some privacy where I could be alone with my thoughts.

I was drawn inexorably toward the grove of mahogany trees. Entering the grove, I found a quietness I had not experienced since leaving home. It felt good to be alone without interruption from anyone. Although the grove was very dense, I noted shafts of sunlight that penetrated the branches and leaves. I felt I was standing on holy ground in a sacred grove, like Joseph Smith. I thought of his experience in his sacred grove and the response he received to his plea for help. That thought drove me to my knees. The tears came freely and I pled with my Father in Heaven to help me overcome the feeling of despair, the foreboding that I might not return from the war. I asked for assurance that I was in the right place doing the right thing for that time of my life. As I prayed, I was reminded it was Christmas Day, a day set aside across the world as a time of peace and good will toward all men, even in time of war. My Savior, Jesus Christ, had lived and died for me. He had never wavered in the face of persecution and despair. He knew of his future, the nature of his impending death, yet he maintained his steady course, his grand mission, teaching by his example as well as precept that he would bring his peace to us.

His words came to my mind: "Peace I leave with you, my peace I give unto you: not as the world giveth, give I unto you. Let not your heart be troubled, neither let it be afraid." (John 14:27.)

As I prayed, I was reminded it was Christmas Day. A comfortable, warm spirit permeated my soul. The darkness left. Fear departed. I felt at peace.

A comfortable, warm spirit permeated my soul. The darkness left. Fear departed. I felt at peace. I felt I was willing to submit my life to my Exemplar and Redeemer. Whatever he required of me I pledged I would do, knowing that he would guide and protect me until my earthly journey was completed. I knew all was well with my loved ones, and that they would be safe from the world until I could return to their sides.

I don't know how long I remained on my knees in that sacred grove. I do know it was the longest, most sincere prayer I had offered to that date.

I walked out of that grove a different man. I returned to the camp renewed and invigorated. Christmas was real. The birth of Jesus Christ assured me that God, our Heavenly Father, rules; that there is a plan of salvation to guide us through this life and back to him; that Jesus Christ is my personal Savior, who died to save me from my sins, to show the way to live in an imperfect world, to show me how to enjoy happiness in the face of all the opposition the world offers to us.

From that day to this I have rejoiced in being a disciple of Jesus Christ!

That memorable Christmas ended on a very happy note. Our fellow servicemen from the navy brought the entire camp a Christmas dinner cooked aboard ship. It included turkey, yams, cranberry sauce, and pumpkin pie.

Boy, did it taste good!

That memorable experience has made every Christmas since then even more meaningful—as I recall the events of that Christmas Day in Hollandia, New Guinea.

ELDER ROBERT L. BACKMAN *was called to be a member of the First Quorum of the Seventy of The Church of Jesus Christ of Latter-day Saints on April 1, 1978, and he was called to serve in the presidency of the quorum in 1985. He was named an emeritus general authority in 1992. Elder Backman is the author of* Take Charge of Your Life *and* Be Master of Yourself.

A Homemade Christmas

Michaelene P. Grassli

CHRISTMAS WAS getting out of hand. Our children were beyond the magical, mysterious secrecy of childhood, yet they seemed to cling to the desire for that aspect of Christmas gift-giving. And so did their parents! It seemed to Leonard and me that it would take an upwardly spiraling cycle of materialism to continue to produce the Christmas morning thrills that had been so easy to achieve with simplicity when the children were small.

Our oldest was married and in college, the second had begun college that year, and the youngest was in junior high. As they had grown up, we had emphasized the significance of the birth of the Savior in our family home evenings and holiday preparations. Leonard always read the Christmas story from Luke on Christmas Eve.

Our ward had initiated a wonderful tradition

where we "returned to Bethlehem" in simple, biblical costumes, ate pita sandwiches, and witnessed the reenactment of the nativity in the cultural hall. About that time, a member of our ward prepared a study guide for twenty-five December family discussions about the prophecies, events, and lessons of the Holy Birth. The ward members gave generously of their means to help less fortunate families.

We had no lack of exposure to the reality of the Savior and to the true reasons for our celebrating his birth. Yet our own family gift-giving seemed to fall somewhat short of the selfless love and generosity we should have been experiencing.

Leonard and I considered this together and decided to introduce an idea to our children. At Thanksgiving dinner we suggested that the gifts we gave to each other for Christmas that year should be something we created ourselves or that were gifts of service. We also suggested that the cost be kept to a minimum. I don't recall whether we named a price limit, but we all knew we needed to be resourceful and conservative.

Our daughters and son-in-law initially were hesitant. School took a big block of their time, and these very personalized gifts would definitely take more time than stopping at the department store downtown and picking up a tie, a pair of gloves, or a sweater. However, after some persuasion and encouragement (after all, we argued, Mom had a demanding Church responsibility,

At Thanksgiving dinner we suggested that the gifts we gave to each other for Christmas that year should be something we created ourselves or that were gifts of service. We also suggested that the cost be kept to a minimum.

and Dad was very busy with work—if we could do it, so could they), they reluctantly agreed.

The days passed, and when I talked to the girls and our son-in-law I would ask how they were coming with ideas. At first they'd roll their eyes and sigh. I'd make some suggestions. Meanwhile, I was sewing, something I had very little time for in those days. I had no idea what Leonard was doing. I must admit to some moments of uneasiness. I saw no evidence of any preparations at all. I really wanted this experiment to succeed and to be a joyous and rewarding time for the family.

Then the mood began to change. The family began to assure me that something really was happening. "Don't ask too many questions, Mom!" they'd say. Our youngest, who was still living at home, seemed more excited about the season than she had been for awhile. My husband just smiled with the knowing twinkle in his eye that he gets when he thinks he's got one on me. The only thing I discovered was that nobody knew what the others were doing. I started to relax as I sewed into the nighttime hours.

Christmas morning came. I don't suppose anyone else would have enjoyed the morning as much as we did, because every gift was so personalized. But enjoy it we did—immensely.

Early in the season our youngest had written on small cards something she loved about each member of the family. She had placed them deep in the toe of each

stocking hung by the fireplace, and her excitement was heightened by the danger that someone might find her notes before Christmas. She told us later that she could hardly wait for Christmas because she was so thrilled with her idea. She said she didn't even wonder what she would receive—a real breakthrough! As it turned out, even Santa did not discover them when he filled the stockings. In addition, she had painted a watercolor of a series of hearts, titling it "Bundle of Love." It still hangs on the wall with our gallery of family photos.

One daughter who has a talent for writing had written a thoughtful and perceptive description of each family member. Another searched carefully for quotes from General Authorities that would be helpful for each family member and their particular challenges at the time. She hand-lettered and matted them. Our son-in-law gave each of us a personalized certificate good for a ski-waxing, which he knew we hadn't had done forever. I sewed I-can't-remember-what for the girls and red Christmas ties for the men.

Leonard is a native of Switzerland (though now he is a U.S. citizen and has lived here longer than he did in Switzerland). His gift to us was a family logo or emblem. His design includes a depiction of the Swiss flag combined with the flag of the United States, his very distinctive Grassli signature, and the date 1412. That is the earliest date we can find the name Grassli recorded in Swiss records. He had the design screen-

I suspect that if we could ask the Savior how he'd like us to celebrate his birthday, he might be pleased with thoughtful gifts that require some sacrifice of time and self.

printed on T-shirts and sweatshirts for us. We all were thrilled with his creation.

All these gifts required thought and perceptivity on the part of family members. They became little labors of love. I suppose others have tried experiments such as this one, but I loved what happened in our family that Christmas. We sort of turned a corner in the way we thought about one another and in how we now prepare for giving gifts at Christmas. That is not to say that we always make everything we give, but we seem to personalize and think about what we do. I suspect that if we could ask the Savior how he'd like us to celebrate his birthday, he might be pleased with thoughtful gifts that require some sacrifice of time and self.

Now that we have two more sons-in-law and six grandchildren, maybe it's time to try it again!

MICHAELENE P. GRASSLI *served as a member of the Primary general board from 1975 to 1980, a counselor in the Primary general presidency from 1980 to 1988, and Primary general president from 1988 to 1994. She is the author or coauthor of three pamphlets and author of two books,* What I Have Learned from Children *and* Leadertalk.

Were You There?

MAURINE JENSEN PROCTOR
AND SCOT FACER PROCTOR

CHRISTMAS EVE *made me breathless when I was a little girl, with almost too much emotion to contain. My mother fluttering in the kitchen and the smell of turkey wafting through the house, the crinkling of wrapping paper behind locked bedroom doors where my sister was wrapping a last surprise, the enchantment of colored Christmas lights reflected in a spray across the living room ceiling. It wasn't just that Santa was coming that night, though it did make the world seem inexpressibly lovely to think that someone invisible to me should know my heart and secret desires, even the ones I hadn't told anyone. "How could Santa know I wanted doll clothes?" I asked my mother, holding up a miniature coat. "Santa just knows," she smiled. What a wonder to be known from the inside out without even having to reveal yourself.*

But Christmas Eve was more to me than even that, something I never told anybody. It ignited a yearn-

ing in me, a longing that was beautiful in itself. I could feel its beauty spread through my system and expand every part. It was a sense of holiness like a memory. What I wanted was the Lord, and it seemed to me that on that night we were all as close as we ever got to having him again.

I had seen nativity scenes acted out, children with crooked halos, shepherds in bathrobes, a mother holding this year's newest infant—but in my child's eye view, I hoped for something more. I thought that on Christmas Eve, somewhere, in some magical way, he must be born again. Maybe it was in Bethlehem a half a world away, where reality might be counted differently than at home. Maybe if you just rounded a corner, like in the movie Brigadoon, *your eyes would clear for a moment and there he'd be, all glowing in his mother's arms. The whole scene would be complete, donkeys and lambs, sweet-smelling straw, shepherds and wise men—and me. He was a little infant, tender and fragile, and I was a little child, tender and fragile too, so we'd have an understanding. I could come right up to him with nobody noticing and say how I felt and not be at all embarrassed: "I love you, Jesus. I miss not seeing you."*

Then enough days passed and I grew up, largely forgetting that I had once thought it possible to visit at the manger.

"You call that work?" our friends would say whenever we were preparing to go on another journey.

"We'll volunteer to come along and just carry the camera bag." These were familiar sentiments to us, for our work as a husband-and-wife creative team has taken us with a camera to the most holy sights of the world to create books about things sacred to us. We have slept at Adam-ondi-Ahman waiting for the first streaks of light across the morning sky, scrambled up Mt. Sinai with a tripod, and tramped through the jungles of Guatemala searching for the best candidate for Zarahemla. But one spring day in Israel stands out above all the rest.

We had wanted our photographs to capture not only the places where significant sacred events had transpired, but also the time and season, bringing the viewer right to the holy place, a participant in the scene. With this in mind, Hill Cumorah had been shot in the fall, memories of young Joseph Smith coming to get plates still lingering in the landscape. We would soon be photographing the Kidron Valley on the night of Passover, the moon casting long shadows across the place where Jesus and his apostles had walked to Gethsemane. But today was April 6, Christ's birthday, and we were on our way to Shepherd's Hill.

"Merry Christmas," we said to each other through tired eyes. It was four o'clock in the morning and still dark outside. When we are on a shoot, we get up morning after morning early enough to beat the sun to the place we are planning to photograph, but we never entirely get used to it. "Anything for a picture," we tell ourselves. "First light is worth it." On this occasion, we awakened Maurine's mother to come with us and the three of us drove through Jerusalem's empty streets, then south of the city to the place where shepherds had once watched their flocks by night and had been awed by a multitude of the heavenly host.

Morning was closer as we pulled our car to the top of the hill, yanked our gear out, and began picking our way across the stony field looking for just the right place to set the camera. Across a little valley about a mile wide, on a hill just opposite where we stood, was Bethlehem, still dark at this early hour. "No one knows this is the real Christmas," we said to each other. "It's like a secret. Everyone is sleeping and they just don't know."

We began to sing, "O little town of Bethlehem, how still we see thee lie." The three of us made a small chorus on the hill and wondered how it was that *we* should be so blessed to know. Where were all the others who could be here celebrating a day of such importance? Our voices were the only sound we heard. "Above thy deep and dreamless sleep the silent stars go by." We ran through our repertoire of carols until we heard the first crowing of the roosters, signaling that dawn was near—and then the hurry, the scramble to have the right lens, the right angle, to be perfectly in focus for the light before it broke across the landscape.

As we were on a northern hill, with Bethlehem on the southwest, the village was the first to catch the light, which then crept slowly toward us. Bit by bit, the

Across a little valley about a mile wide, on a hill just opposite where we stood, was Bethlehem, still dark at this early hour. We began to sing, "O little town of Bethlehem, how still we see thee lie." The three of us made a small chorus on the hill.

scene which had been painted in hues of gray and blue became illuminated. Then we could see ambling stone walls, the caves that pocked the hillsides. The colors changed, the rock houses of Bethlehem becoming amber in the sun, the hills brushed with dusty olive. Bright red poppies, which had been closed in the cool night, now stretched open to the light.

Of course it would have been like this, we thought—of course his birth would be in the spring, a season of new life. He had told us that "all things are created and made to bear record" of him (Moses 6:63), so no other season would do. The image of a snowy Christmas where your breath hangs like a cloud in the air before you and the ground is thick with snow was quickly slipping away. The shepherds had been out watching their flocks by night because it was the season of new lambs that needed their special protection. The earth was green and growing again after its little season of death to symbolize him who came to give life more abundantly. Of course his birth was in the spring.

God reveals himself to us not just in words, but also through the earth itself and the very shape our experience takes. It is as if all things, including the events in our lives, are constantly pushing on our spirits, saying, "See. See. Here is a type of Christ—but only if you have eyes to see." Here we were in Bethlehem, where the very land echoes with his presence, where his image is in every rock and tree, and we could see the witnesses everywhere.

Here we were in Bethlehem, where the very land echoes with his presence, where his image is in every rock and tree, and we could see the witnesses everywhere. "It was like this," we thought, "just like this."

The word *Bethlehem* itself means "House of Bread" in Hebrew, and he came to be the bread of life. Bread is the perfect symbol to speak to us needy mortals, who get our fill of bread only to need it once again. Then, too, Bethlehem was the home of David, the shepherd who was also a king. From Bethlehem flowed the waters that quenched the thirst of all Jerusalem, and Christ was the living water. Even the fields crusted by stones were a symbol of him and celebrated his coming. "Wherefore, I am in your midst, and I am the good shepherd, and the stone of Israel." (D&C 50:44.) We saw him on the left and on the right, before us and behind us.

With the light came the early morning sounds. His newborn cry must have carried on the air with noises just like these. Sheep were bleating on the hillsides, birds sang, dogs barked, and somewhere across the way a stubborn donkey who didn't want to start a day of work was braying his complaint. These were rural sounds, village noises, sounds of life spilling into the air that hadn't changed in two thousand years. "It was like this," we thought, "just like this." No hush for his coming. No pause in the routine. People went on about their work, unnoticing. He added his baby cry to a thousand sounds to join us in life. If we listened hard enough even now, we could probably hear a baby cry.

We took our pictures, moved the camera to a different angle and snapped again, but the images printed on our souls were the most vivid—a scene bearing record of him. It would have been gift enough had the day ended there, but there was more.

Photographers don't usually take pictures during the flat light of day. Our work is accomplished in the first light of morning and the last light of night. Noon offers no shadows or plays of light, no nuances that make a picture sing. So that late afternoon we came back to the same spot to complete our shot list. We needed to get a photograph of a flock of sheep; we hoped to snap a picture of a little lamb—a picture we had been after for weeks. Lambs don't cooperate, fleeing in terror before the camera. We had spent the afternoon buying ten small, olive oil lamps, and once it got dark, we hoped to light them and take a picture to illustrate the parable of the ten virgins. Finally, we hoped to get a night shot of Bethlehem, nestled on the hill under starry skies.

The sheep were first on the list. The sun was low in the sky as we scrambled over one stone wall with our gear and then sat on another, watching a family of Bedouins tending their flocks. Suddenly we heard an explosion, felt the ground rumble, and quickly turned to the east to see smoke rising from the trees. Our mother and our daughter Laura, who were resting in the car, had heard the sound too. "That must have been a sonic boom," they said almost simultaneously, each hoping the other would be comforted by the bad guess. It hadn't been. A mortar shell had landed a few hundred yards away, and though it may have been just a military maneuver, it was a grim reminder that this place where the Prince of Peace had been born was in turmoil, a land divided, where even teachers of schoolchildren carry machine guns to guard the students, and the military is a constant presence. Was it safe to stay for our pictures? Should we go? But this was April 6 and we had pictures yet to take. A little shaken, we turned back to the sheep, who grazed in friendly clusters before us.

We took several pictures of the sheep, the wooly silhouette of their bodies outlined in flame in the setting sun. One little lamb pulled away from the flock, scampered up a rocky ledge and turned back long enough for a photograph.

Sheep are helpless creatures, without defenses, unable to protect themselves against roaming wolves or nighttime predators. God gave porcupines quills and cheetahs speed, but sheep he left vulnerable. They are perfect symbols for humanity without the Lord. That is why they need a good shepherd who will stay with them in all kinds of weather and at nighttime lead them into a fold and sleep across its only gate. Burned by the sun and parched in the wind, the shepherd's job isn't glamorous or even very picturesque, but the sheep cannot survive without him. He is good; he is constant. His sheep know his voice when he calls them forth again in the morning. Even if several flocks are tended together in one fold, the sheep will respond only to the voice of their master.

So our eyes scanned the hills for a shepherd to

Sheep are helpless creatures, unable to protect themselves against roaming predators. They are perfect symbols for humanity without the Lord. They need a good shepherd who will stay with them.

Flocks of sheep were folded in some of these caves at night, and once, somewhere near here, Christ was born in this kind of stable. His manger was not wooden, but made of stone, a feeding trough for animals.

see what we could learn, finally fixing on a bearded man in a flowing robe carrying a lamb tenderly close to his chest, his arms wrapped around the little creature. We watched the lamb with some affection and wondered: Had this lamb strayed, been lost? The man picked his way with sandaled feet carefully across the stony hillside, down a slope and back up again, past the tent of his family to the wall where we sat.

Then in an instant the image changed. Now we were no longer being taught about the Good Shepherd. He was gone. Instead we were shown why Christ was the Lamb. The Bedouin brought the submissive lamb, laid it gently on a rock, and then with a swift stroke, he slit its throat. Tonight was their holy feast, and a lamb was needed. It was a shocking moment, completely unexpected, the reality of sacrifice suddenly vivid and graphic before us, no longer comfortably removed into a clean and sterile abstraction. The lamb's blood spurted and splattered and then flowed freely. Then when the little creature had squealed and struggled its last, the Bedouin tied the body to the stone wall just a few hundred feet from us. Poor little lamb. We were drawn both to look and to turn away, but turning away conquered as the wall became flooded and stained red.

Here was a lamb that had gone willingly to the slaughter. For us, it had become more than a creature of the earth. It had become the Lamb who had also gone willingly, who had suffered for our sins, "Which suffering caused myself, even God, the greatest of all, to tremble because of pain, and to bleed at every pore, and to suffer both body and spirit—and would that I might not drink the bitter cup, and shrink." (D&C 19:18.) Would we ever be able to think about the atonement the same way again? Could we comfortably distance ourselves from it? We couldn't take a picture of the scene before us. Something about it was much too sacred.

It seemed a good moment to grab our camera and explore, probe some of the shallow caves that dotted the hillside. Flocks of sheep were folded in some of these caves at night, and once, somewhere near here, Christ was born in this kind of stable. His manger was not wooden, but made of stone, a feeding trough for animals. The sun set while we were in a cave, and we pointed our camera toward the last light, using the cave as a frame. Was it a night like this when Nephi, a continent away, had been told that Christ would be born? "Lift up your head and be of good cheer; for behold, the time is at hand, and on this night shall the sign be given, and on the morrow come I into the world." (3 Nephi 1:13.)

By now the sun had fallen behind the western horizon, and it was dark enough to photograph the glow from ten oil lamps. Mother and Laura brought them from the car, and together we set them on an ancient olive press. We had spent several days trying to figure out the best way to photograph these lamps. We couldn't do it in our little room in the kibbutz, lest we set the place on fire. Besides, light pink walls seemed like an odd backdrop for an oil lamp. We couldn't shoot them on a wall in the city with the glow of traffic lights nearby. Finally we had determined to bring them to this isolated spot, so whatever background showed in the picture beyond them would be authentic. But lighting them was another problem. We rolled cotton into makeshift wicks and filled each lamp with olive oil. Scot was poised and ready behind the camera for the moment.

"Okay, let's do it," Scot said. Mother and Maurine each struck a match and started at either end of the row, quickly lighting the lamps. We were looking for the lamps to burn for thirty to sixty seconds because a nighttime exposure, even for a picture of a flame, is a long exposure. But the cotton was slow to catch fire and wouldn't stay lit. Though we worked quickly, two matches were not enough. "We've got one virgin lamp going, two virgin lamps, three . . . four, five, no, four." With the cooling of the evening, a slight breeze began to blow—just enough to make some of the lamps flicker and die. "Three virgin lamps, two . . . oh no! They're all out."

We struck our matches and began the process again, Scot ready with his finger on the shutter. "Hurry, hurry. Tell me when you're ready."

"Okay, now there's four virgin lamps, five, six, seven, eight, no, six." Some of the wicks just wouldn't light. Others glowed for a second and then sputtered out. We tried to use our bodies as a wind shield. That didn't work. We tried to use our camera bag as a wind shield. That didn't work. "You know we really don't need ten virgin lights. Only five of them had enough oil. We should have thought of that before." Good idea. We hoped we could succeed with a more realistic number.

Even five turned out to be impossible. About the sixth time through the lighting process, with the lamps flickering in turn and then dying, Maurine said, "This concept is all wrong. I'm sure this isn't the way they did it. We have to give up. We'll never get a time exposure of five lamps all lit at the same time." Our thoughts went to the foolish virgins with new sympathy. "Give us of your oil; for our lamps are gone out." (Matthew 25:8.)

"There's a way to do this and we won't give up." It was Mom speaking with the same determination we had seen before. "Who said it would be okay to give up?" She made new wicks, passed out several matches, and told us how to line up as a wind shield. "Now, Scot, be ready on the camera. Let's go." Laughing, we lit the lamps and Scot began the time exposure.

Five virgin lights; no, four; no, three. Yes, three. Three stayed lit for the entire exposure, but before we could enjoy the moment, something happened that we wouldn't have believed had we not all stood there to witness it.

Hearing a hollow boom, we turned away from the lamps and back toward Bethlehem, whose lights now made it glow on the hillside. And there above the city, the most visible thing in the nighttime sky was a new star. It was glistening there like every Christmas

There above the city, the most visible thing in the nighttime sky was a new star. It was glistening there like every Christmas picture we'd ever seen of it, lighting the way to the manger.

In a way I couldn't quite explain, the nativity and the atonement both happened again for me that day. I had been there. I had seen it all enacted again, felt it in my bones and sinews.

picture we'd ever seen of it, lighting the way to the manger. Since we were alone on Shepherd's Hill, it couldn't have seemed more personal, more designed for our own wonder on this April 6. "It's the star. It's the star," we cried. "For we have seen his star in the east, and are come to worship him." (Matthew 2:2.) We felt loved and noticed by the heavens, invited to the manger, not just for this evening, but for always. We had always loved the French nativity sets where more than just the shepherds and wise men have come to the stable. In them, all the townsfolk are invited, the cripple with his crutch, the newlyweds, the elderly, the merchant and stone mason. Tonight we were invited by our own star.

Though our bright star was only a military flare, to have it shot into the sky that night seemed more than coincidental. It completed our picture as it hovered over Bethlehem for some time. Had we paid a special effects team to create the picture for us, it couldn't have more perfectly fit our imagined picture of the event. We could have hardly been more taken if we had seen the actual star two thousand years ago. We took a photograph of it, but the film could not capture the wonder of the moment. Being a long time exposure, it revealed what our eyes couldn't see—that the "star" was imperceptibly drifting down, leaving a trail of light behind it. We live in a weary world where sometimes stars don't stay.

But I wanted the star to stay, wanted all the symbols that had been pressed upon my soul that day to stay,

like an engraving. Then I knew that sometimes children know more than adults, that all those years ago I had been right on Christmas Eve when I had thought that somewhere, somehow Christ was born again on that night. For in a way I couldn't quite explain, the nativity and the atonement both happened again for me that day. I had been there. I had seen it all enacted again, felt it in my bones and sinews. And I felt to exclaim, "Shine for me, star of Bethlehem. Always shine on for me."

MAURINE AND SCOT PROCTOR *are a husband-and-wife creative team who have photographed many of the sacred sites of the world for their books* Witness of the Light, Source of the Light, Light from the Dust, *and* The Gathering—Mormon Pioneers on the Trail to Zion. *Former editors of* This People *magazine, their films and documentaries have won several awards. They are both part-time Institute teachers.*

The Gift-Giver

JANATH R. CANNON

CHRISTMAS OF 1938 was not a festive time in Germany. Indeed, the events of that whole year would mark it as one of the darkest in history. On February 4, Adolf Hitler had assumed command of the Third Reich's military machine, which then proceeded to take over the bordering countries of Austria and Czechoslovakia. An uneasy quiet followed Hitler's diplomatic triumph at the Munich Conference in September, where France's Daladier and England's Chamberlain had put the Czechs in Hitler's grasp for the sake of "peace in our time."

That fragile quiet was shattered with the sound of glass being broken across the land on the night of November 19. Using as an excuse the murder of a German diplomat in France, supposedly by a Jew, the Nazis unleashed their war against all the Jews. A young American missionary for The Church of Jesus Christ of

Latter-day Saints, Elder Edwin Q. Cannon Jr. (known as Ted), who was stationed in northern Germany, recorded his shock in his journal:

"All night long there was much disturbance. We awoke in the morning to find the Jewish synagogue burned right to the ground and stores destroyed with the windows broken in. . . . This movement took place throughout entire Germany. In Berlin, President Rees said, they mobbed all Jewish stores. On Kurfursten-damm, the swankiest street in Europe, all of the won-derful stores were destroyed. . . . Jews just *disappeared?* during the night.

"I can see government's slow strangling process on all sides. . . . One can also see the movement by the churches and the people as a whole to first throw off the Old Testament and then the New Testament even to throwing off Jesus, as he was a 'Jew.'"

Truly, 1938 was not an auspicious year in Germany to celebrate the Savior's birth. Yet in spite of the evil abroad in the land, Christmas was coming. Ted looked forward to it eagerly, for he had been invited to accompany his companion, Tom McKay, to Switzer-land, where Tom's father, Thomas E. McKay, was the mission president. Switzerland was an island of peace in Europe's stormy sea; the mission home would be a haven of family love and familiar Christmas joys, a place to gather strength for the difficult year ahead.

But President Rees had other plans for him. A new missionary in the north needed help in his struggle

to learn German and overcome homesickness; his companion also needed help. A strong companion for the two of them was the president's solution. Ted's journal reveals no hint of the disappointment he must have felt at the call:

"Brother McKay went to Switzerland to visit his folks there and we said goodbye and I went my way. In Insterburg I stayed with brother Evans and his companion. My job was to help them out in any way I could. I started out by helping brother Evans study German."

Christmas came without fanfare, but not without the Spirit. Ted recorded nothing of church or community Christmas decorations or programs, nor of gifts received or given. But nature's lavish decorating skills were noted, and the gifts he gave to others are visible in his journal:

"On Christmas Eve it started to snow and it was really beautiful. We had a long walk through town in this snow-storm and I had a wonderful feeling. We sang 'Silent Night' and other Xmas carols all the way and had a wonderful time. . . . Monday we went to a little dorf called Sobrost to visit a family Braun. There was a wonderful spirit in the home. We played, talked and ate with them for three days. I slept between two big Goosedown ticks in an ice-cold room. We ate Schweinebraten because they had just killed a pig for Christmas."

The Braun family members were Latter-day

Saints with a missionary spirit. They invited their farmer neighbors from all around to a house-meeting with their American guests. Ted wrote about the meeting:

"I read the shepherd verses from Luke's Gospel while brother Braun played 'Silent Night' on his violin—I surely felt the Spirit when I did that. I then gave a speech about Christmas. How Augustus called a census of the whole world, and as Mary & Joseph went to this census, there was at the same time, in a 'world' that was not included in this census, a prophet on his knees in prayer. (3 Nephi 1.) I told of the happening in both hemispheres that night."

Outside, the Baltic wind moaned in the bare trees as the pale horse bearing Death and War galloped ever nearer. But inside the crowded cottage, the candles on a small Christmas tree lit the faces of those who listened attentively as the young missionary spoke. "It was the best speech I have ever given," he wrote in the journal with ingenuous satisfaction—and perhaps a little awe.

A few days later, a journal entry records an even more touching success:

"In helping brother Evans prepare a speech, I started talking about a testimony. I talked [with him] for about three hours and the whole time there were tears in Brother Evans' eyes. We finally ended up that a testimony of the Gospel is the only sure thing that we can stand on in this unsure world. . . . In the afternoon of the same day, he started to read his patriarchal blessing to

Outside, the Baltic wind moaned in the bare trees as the pale horse bearing Death and War galloped ever nearer. But inside, the candles on a small Christmas tree lit the faces of those who listened as the young missionary spoke.

me but broke down. I took it and read it to him, after which he asked me to join him in prayer. He prayed & then I prayed. . . . We stood up feeling lots better. Bro. Evans was very earnest and will work until he gets the language."

One year later, with all the missionaries either released or transferred from Europe to safer missions, a Christmas greeting reached Elder Cannon in the Canadian mission home from Elder Sterling Evans in Minnesota:

"Dear Ted, Christmas brought back vivid memories of a year ago. I will always be indebted to you; because of me, you missed seeing Switzerland and association with the McKays. . . . Tomorrow I receive my 4th new companion since I've been here! President Broadbent said that he was using me as a trainer of Elders. . . . If I have pleased him by my efforts, it is largely due to the splendid help you gave to me one year ago."

Elder Evans had no immediate need for the German language on which he had worked so hard, but the gifts of faith and testimony he had received were of everlasting worth. He would never forget that Christmas in northern Germany—nor would the missionary who cheerfully gave up his Christmas in Switzerland to help him.

Thirty-three years later, Edwin Q. Cannon Jr. became the president of the Switzerland Mission and spent three Christmases there.

A MORE PERSONAL GIFT

That Christmas of 1939 in the Canadian mission home was also memorable for me, for I too received a priceless gift from Elder Cannon. I was there as a refugee from the French Mission—the last full-time lady missionary to leave Europe, so far as I know—waiting for a companion and a new place to start missionary work. Meanwhile, I helped in the office and was grateful to be part of President and Sister David A. Smith's mission home family.

Canada was involved in the war effort as part of the British Commonwealth; the prevailing atmosphere was a brave "Keep a stiff upper lip." I had grown up hearing that the next big war would surely be the last, as eventually no one would be left to do the fighting. Of course, only a madman would start such a war—and now Hitler had done it! I had been part of the fearful preparations in Paris after war was declared—the blackout, the gas masks, sirens in the night that sent us stumbling down four dangerous flights of curving stairs to the basement shelter. It was a scary time I could not forget.

Elder Cannon had arrived in Canada weeks before me and was diligently pursuing his missionary labors in Kitchener when he broke his leg on Thanksgiving Day. Kind President Smith decided to bring him into the mission home to recuperate. His presence added a surprising amount of cheer to the somewhat gloomy atmosphere. He joked about his

I was there as a refugee from the French Mission—the last full-time lady missionary to leave Europe, so far as I know—waiting for a companion and a new place to start missionary work.

heavy cast and awkward crutches as he climbed the two flights of stairs to the elders' attic bedroom. He knelt comically on one knee at morning prayers, with his cast sticking out to one side. He could also be serious. When it was his turn to pray, I noticed with approval that he remembered the suffering people of Europe—especially the Jews. (Two of my best friends in high school were Jewish.)

One evening just before Christmas we all went to a neighborhood movie theater. I don't remember the movie, just the Hollywood cartoon—a grandfather squirrel telling the little ones about the terrible humans who used to terrorize the planet, before they destroyed each other. One of the last scenes printed itself indelibly on my mind: the last two humans, in gas masks and battle dress, rising out of opposite trenches, killing each other with machine guns. Could this be the way the world would end in the last days—and were those days already upon us? It was definitely not a happy thought for Christmas!

We walked back to the mission home through falling snow. There, hot spiced cider and doughnuts warmed us, and lights twinkled on the Christmas tree. The office elders enjoyed their usual good-natured banter. But I sat apart, looking into the little gas fireplace and brooding. Quietly, Elder Cannon came to perch on a footstool beside me; quietly, he put his hand over mine, smiling reassuringly as if he understood my sad thoughts. And suddenly the sad thoughts were

The office elders enjoyed their usual good-natured banter. But I sat apart, looking into the little gas fireplace and brooding.

gone. Hope and courage seemed to flow from his warm hand. I smiled back.

On Christmas morning we opened our presents. My gift from the mission home family was a book I still treasure: *Jesus the Christ,* by James E. Talmage. The signatures of the gift-givers are on the front page—headed by "Edwin Q. Cannon, Jr. (Ted)"—my now and forever husband.

JANATH RUSSELL CANNON, *who served as first counselor to Barbara B. Smith in the Relief Society general presidency, has taught at the University of Utah and written extensively on Church history. A former member of the Tabernacle Choir, she has served as matron of the Frankfurt Germany Temple and on missionary assignments in four continents with her husband, Edwin Q. Cannon Jr. She is coauthor of* Women of Covenant.

Christmas through a Window of Time

FRANCIS M. GIBBONS

LOOK WITH ME through a window of time to see a Christmas in another era, a Christmas in southern Utah in 1935. . . .

The Bays loved Christmas. Indeed, they cherished it above all other holidays. Even the Fourth of July, with the excitement of fireworks and footraces, stood a distant second in their feelings.

The reasons for the bias are clear. The father of the family, H. Earl Bay, was the bishop of the Junction, Utah, Ward. His compassionate nature and spirituality imbued his family with a love for the Savior and an understanding of the significance of Christmas.

The mother, Iola Maxwell Bay, was the guardian of the family Christmas traditions. She organized the holiday arrangements, prepared the food, decorated the house and the Christmas tree, and checked to be sure everyone was remembered with suitable gifts in sufficient numbers. Iola had a beautiful round face, set off by rosy cheeks and laughing eyes that threw off sparkles when she smiled. By picturing some false padding, one could easily think of her as the embodiment of an imaginary Mrs. Santa Claus.

The influence of these parents, and the rich traditions the family had nurtured, endowed Christmas with an almost magical quality for the Bay children. Feelings of excitement were generated weeks before the event and lingered afterward like the remembered strains of a beautiful melody.

In December of 1935, Earl and Iola had six children. Two more were born later. The oldest, Helen, buoyant and imaginative, could captivate her young siblings and their friends with fanciful tales. She was an "almost mother" to the younger Bay children—feeding, bathing, and diapering them as necessary. Bernice, bouncy and mischievous, was two years younger than Helen. As a little girl, she could coerce her older sister into doing her will by threatening to let the coyotes get her. Bud, the oldest son, was four years younger than Bernice. When he was a small child, Bud thought he became invisible on closing his eyes. He would feel his way into Earl's confectionery and grope toward the candy, confident he could not be seen. Later he was amazed at his mother's perceptiveness when she knew he had taken an unauthorized swim because his hair was wet and his clothes dry. Mary Lorraine, two years younger than Bud, was the pretty and caring friend to

all. Three-year-old Elvon, blond and full of bravado, was prone to wander, unless closely guarded or tethered. And baby Paul was only five months old.

At Christmas 1935, the Bays had felt the pinch of the Great Depression. Earl was pressed to provide for his large and growing family. The income from his job as postmaster was insufficient. He supplemented it with income from several sidelines: He converted a room adjoining the post office into a combined store and confectionery where he sold homemade ice cream, candy, canned goods, and nonprescription drugs; he operated Earl's Auto Camp, which consisted of several rustic cabins he built from materials salvaged from old houses he had purchased and razed; he sold hunting licenses, was the ticket agent for the bus line, and was a representative of the power company; and he pumped and sold Parco gas. Moreover, he was a skilled carpenter whose services were often in demand in Junction and nearby communities. He was a careful craftsman, insisting that everything be plumb, with lines straight and edges smooth. His painstaking habits irritated some customers who lacked his eye for detail and were interested only in seeing the job finished quickly. He never compromised, however, and insisted that the work be done right, even though it required that he devote time for which he received no payment and involved the risk of alienating a customer. "If you don't have time to do it right the first time," he would say, "how will you *ever* find time to do it again?"

Obviously, Bishop Bay was unable to do all that work himself. He relied heavily on Iola and the older children for help. Except for the carpentry, these duties became a family enterprise. Whoever was available distributed the mail, tended the store and confectionery, rented rooms to tourists, sold bus tickets, pumped Parco gas, issued hunting permits, or received utility payments.

Much of this burden fell on Iola. When added to her other duties as wife, mother, homemaker, and hostess to many visitors (including General Authorities who always stayed at the bishop's home), she had little leisure. The Christmas events threw her schedule into overload.

Earl and Iola began their Christmas preparations early. Lacking surplus money, many gifts were homemade. Earl fashioned many toys and pieces of furniture for the children and the family. A three-wheeled kiddy car, fondly named Freda, was enjoyed by the Bay children for many years. A high chair, now in the possession of one of Earl's grandsons, was constructed to be used not only as a chair, but also as a teeter-totter, a slippery slide, a wheel-less car (propelled by the humming noises of the driver), and, when turned on its side, as a small serving table. He also made major pieces of furniture which are now family heirlooms—tables, chairs, and a buffet. The Bay children remember there was often a faint odor of paint on Christmas morning, since the new toys had not had time to dry fully in

An unexpected telephone call shattered her sense of peace. She reacted instantly and decisively. "Bud," she called, "go fill up the car with Parco. We're going to go get Helen in Cedar City."

Earl's car shed. Meanwhile, Iola added to the cache of gifts by sewing clothes and preparing special candies and pastries.

On the day before Christmas in 1935, the preparations were almost completed. Earlier, the beautiful tree had been cut on the mountain west of town, up toward Puffer Lake. It was adorned with the traditional decorations, and gifts had begun to mound around the base of it. Earl had gone to a nearby town to perform a piece of emergency carpentry, and Iola was happily engrossed in making final preparations. An unexpected telephone call shattered her sense of peace. It was from a friend across the mountain who said he would not be driving to Junction as planned and that he could not give Helen a ride. She had been attending school in Cedar City that semester, living with an aunt and uncle. The thought that Helen would be away from her family at Christmas devastated Iola. She reacted instantly and decisively. "Bud," she called, "go fill up the car with Parco. We're going to go get Helen in Cedar City."

The car was a Model-A Ford, serviceable but not fancy. Eight-year-old Bud was selected to go with his mother so she would have a "man" along in case of car trouble. This flattery seems to have been a subterfuge to mask the reality that Iola wanted to get Bud out of Bernice's hair, since Bernice would be in charge of the family and the Bay compound in her absence.

It was not a good day to drive over the mountain. Snow had fallen several days before, and the

It was not a good day to drive over the mountain. Snow had fallen several days before, and the unsurfaced road was a conglomerate of ice, snow, and mud. Things became especially treacherous when they left Highway 89.

unsurfaced road was a conglomerate of ice, snow, and mud. Things became especially treacherous when they left Highway 89 south of Circleville to go westward through Bear Valley toward Highway 91. Iola thought it strange that they passed no oncoming traffic after the cutoff. The mystery was solved when at the junction with Highway 91 she found a "Road Closed" sign. The highway department had failed to post a similar sign on the east side of the mountain.

Meanwhile, in Cedar City, Helen had arisen early, excited at the prospect of going home for Christmas. Perhaps the most ardent "Christmas person" among the Bay children, she had never been away from home during the holidays. She had packed her things and sat waiting for the promised ride, a suitcase at her side. Unaware of the change in plans, she began to worry when her ride didn't show on time. Worry turned to anxiety as the minutes ticked on. She could never quite describe her feeling of relief and utter joy when she saw her mother and Bud pull up in front of Aunt Theresa's house. The old Model-A never looked so good.

They drove home via Clear Creek Canyon north of Junction, which was a longer but safer route. They arrived home in the late afternoon. In the meantime, Earl had returned home and had completed the plans for the annual ward Christmas party in Junction's little chapel. There was the usual appearance of Santa Claus with gifts for the children, caroling, and a Christmas story.

But it was later, in the warmth and glow of the family home, surrounding the tree piled with gifts, that the Bays truly enjoyed the spirit of Christmas. There, as they knelt in family prayer, Earl gave thanks for life's bounties and for the priceless gift of the Savior, whose birth they celebrated.

But that wasn't the end of it, of course. The younger children still anticipated Santa's annual visit to the Bay home. According to tradition, a piece of pie and a glass of milk were left out as a treat for the rotund visitor. Being the oldest child, Helen was privileged to stay up to help retrieve from their hiding place the gifts Earl and Iola had lovingly made, and to arrange them around the tree. Helen ate the treat and left a note, "Thanks, from Santa."

As that Christmas Eve closes, our window on the past closes as well. But that's not the end of the story.

Many of the traditions and the love for Christmas generated in the family of H. Earl Bay and Iola Maxwell Bay have found their way into the family of the writer and his wife, Helen Bay Gibbons. Changes in lifestyle and economic conditions, the writer's abysmal lack of carpentry skills, and personal innovations have necessarily altered the procedures and the format of the Christmas celebration as observed in the Gibbons family.

She had packed her things and sat waiting for the promised ride, a suitcase at her side. But she began to worry when her ride didn't show on time. Worry turned to anxiety as the minutes ticked on.

But one thing has not changed. Helen has ever remained completely dedicated to the idea of giving and sharing at Christmastime, in the spirit of the Savior. This is something she learned in the home of her parents, parents who had little in the way of earthly wealth, but who lavished all they had on their children. And in that giving, Earl and Iola Bay created an example that will endure, for we see much of the same attitude and style in the families of our children. Their children will likely follow the same pattern—the goodness of Christmas, a sweet remembrance of our Savior, passed on from generation to generation without end.

ELDER FRANCIS M. GIBBONS *served as secretary to the First Presidency for sixteen years under four different prophets. He was called to the First Quorum of the Seventy in April 1986, the Second Quorum of the Seventy in April 1989, and was released as a General Authority in October 1991. He is the author of biographies of nearly all the presidents of the Church, the most recent being* Spencer W. Kimball: Resolute Disciple, Prophet of God.

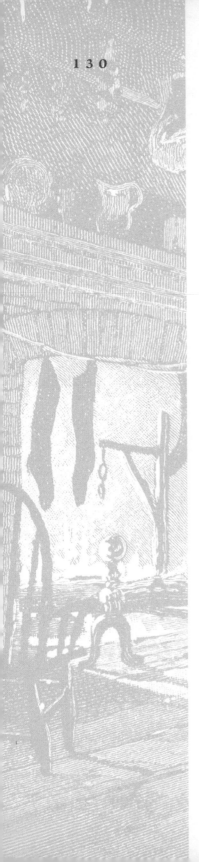

Stomach Flu
Christmas

JANENE WOLSEY BAADSGAARD

MY MOST MEMORABLE Christmas was the one I now affectionately call the stomach flu Christmas. Six weeks before that cold Christmas Eve, I had given birth to my son Jacob. This pregnancy had been particularly long and difficult because my doctor had ordered bed rest to prevent Jacob's premature delivery. After seven pregnancies in eight years, this Christmas season found me exhausted and discouraged. It seemed I didn't have the time, health, or money to do the things I thought were truly important for the kind of Christmas I wanted my children to have.

I truly wanted the picture-perfect Christmas I'd seen in Hollywood movies or read about in books. But a postpartum bleeding problem, a lingering infection, and a house full of overactive young children all left me feeling chronically overwhelmed. After paying off the doctors and hospital, we didn't have much money left over

for gifts. I'd been sewing dolls from cloth scraps and painting blocks and toy trucks from leftover wood ends in the wee hours between late-night feedings and other fussy sessions with my newborn son.

Then on Christmas Eve, it hit like a blast of arctic air . . . the dreaded stomach flu. All my children suddenly became violently ill. They were too young or too weak to reach the bathroom, so I rushed from bed to crib diapering, changing sheets, and comforting the best I could.

Then the illness hit me just as hard. I soon found myself unable to stand without fainting—which thing I learned the hard way. I must have hit my head on the corner of our nightstand passing out, because my forehead was throbbing and a lump was forming when I woke up on the floor in my bedroom.

For a moment I lay motionless on the floor, paralyzed with nausea, cramping, and throbbing pain. Then I tried to figure out what I should do. If I called someone for help, I would expose friends or family to the dangerous condition of the ice-covered roads and this awful illness. My husband had been out of town on a business trip and should have been home hours ago. Because he hadn't called, I worried he might be stranded on the road somewhere or in an accident.

I felt so sick, alone, and afraid.

"Mom! Mom! Help me!" I heard my children crying and retching in their rooms.

"Dear Father in Heaven," I prayed. "Why does

everything have to be so hard, especially on Christmas Eve?"

"Mommy! I need you!"

"Please give me the strength," I prayed. "My children need me."

I raised my head and felt another fainting spell coming on, so I maneuvered my body into a kneeling position. If I kept my head down, I could slowly crawl from bed to bed. Hours passed with no break.

Around midnight, I heard the front door open and my husband trudging toward the back of the house. I was lying in a near-fetal position on the floor in the hallway, remaining next to the children's bedrooms so I could hear and respond to their needs. My newborn son, Jacob, was wrapped in a blanket and cradled in the bend of my body. My husband rushed into the bathroom, then to the bedroom, where he collapsed on the bed and moaned. He wouldn't be able to help. He was as sick as the rest of us.

Just then I heard the pendulum clock in the family room begin the first of twelve soft chimes. When the clock grew silent, I knew Christmas had come. I didn't have the strength to put gifts under the tree and the stockings were still empty, but my children were sleeping peacefully for the first time that evening. I felt the slow gentle breaths of my infant son on my neck. Clouds parted in the night sky outside just enough to let a faint bit of moonlight filter into the hallway.

"It's Christmas," I thought.

I raised my head and felt another fainting spell coming on, so I maneuvered my body into a kneeling position. If I kept my head down, I could slowly crawl from bed to bed. Hours passed with no break.

Then, as if someone had quietly placed a blanket fresh from the dryer all around me, I felt instantly warm. I remembered another mother and child . . . another Christmas when everything didn't work out as planned . . . a Christmas when all the inns were full, when the Savior of the world, Creator and Almighty God, was born in a stable because there was no room.

I knew that babe in the manger was my personal Savior. I knew I was loved and that I was not alone. Christ understood my situation because he had experienced all that I was feeling personally. He would never leave me comfortless.

I will never forget the stomach flu Christmas. It taught me that life seldom works out the way we plan—and that is the wonder of it all. For only in sickness and pain are we awake to the gift of health and love. The stomach flu Christmas taught me that God wants me to grow up, to understand that life is supposed to be a series of problems, even on Christmas Eve; for pain opens the door to understanding. It taught my children that they have a mother who loves them. Perhaps that deep, abiding love was the greatest gift I had to offer. Maybe what I had to give my children wasn't Hollywood . . . but it was real.

Other Christmas Eves have come and gone with the more common, frantic preparations for that much awaited morning, but the stomach flu Christmas stands out because I know now there is joy even in sorrow . . . that the daily miracles of life, health, love, and family should not be taken for granted, not even for a moment. In the stillness of that night, I learned that only in darkness does the light and love of the Savior shine brightest.

JANENE WOLSEY BAADSGAARD *is the author of six books, including* Families Who Laugh . . . Last, Why Does My Mother's Day Potted Plant Always Die?, *and* Family Finances for the Flabbergasted. *She has been home and family editor for the* Utah County Journal *and family life columnist for the* Deseret News. *In addition, she has written numerous feature articles for the* New Era *and the* Ensign *magazines. She teaches writing and literature classes at Utah Valley State College. She is the mother of eight children.*

Paul's Gift

DEANNA EDWARDS

IT WAS CHRISTMAS DAY. An icy wind blew a few of the last brown leaves across the frozen snowdrifts, leaving bare trees to cast a pattern against the cold blue sky. It felt good to be inside where it was warm and cozy, but I couldn't shake the feeling that I was needed at the hospital. I kept thinking that if I found it delightful to be at home with Cliff, the children, and soft Christmas lights, how lonely it must be for some of the patients who couldn't go home for Christmas for even a few minutes.

I called to Cliff, who was in the living room. "Honey, would it be all right with you if I go to the hospital for a while this afternoon?"

After a brief silence, he called back, "Deanna, do you feel you have to go today? Christmas is a family day. Couldn't you go tomorrow?"

I walked into the living room, and his eyes met

Outlined against the window, a man sat on the edge of his bed smoking a cigarette. There was not a sign of Christmas anywhere in his room. The only possession he seemed to have in the world was his cigarette.

mine. "Cliff, I don't know why. I just feel there's someone in the hospital today who needs me."

Cliff's voice softened as he sensed the urgency in my voice. "If you feel it's important, then you should go." He smiled. "Just don't be gone too long."

I often visited the hospital, singing to cheer up patients at a difficult time in their lives. This day the hospital was unusually quiet, with only a few staff members on duty. A Christmas tree stood in the waiting room, its drooping branches tied with bright red bows. Most of the patients who were not seriously ill had been released so they could spend the day with their families, and I noticed many empty beds in the rooms as I walked down the hallway on the main floor.

I entered the elevator, wondering where I should go first, and, without thinking, pushed the third-floor button. Room 381, next to the nurses' station, is one I will never forget. It was dimly lit by the fading afternoon sun. Outlined against the window, a man sat on the edge of his bed smoking a cigarette. There was not a sign of Christmas anywhere in his room. No sprig of holly or bright ornament. No Christmas cards or gifts. The only possession he seemed to have in the world was his cigarette. I looked into his thin, gray face and judged him to be in his early sixties. The veins stood out above his temples, accentuated by his baldness. A white hospital gown was draped about his slight form.

The patient's face registered surprise and curios-

ity when I entered his room, and I could hear the unspoken question, *What are you doing here?*

"I'm a volunteer at the hospital," I said, "and I thought some of the patients would like to hear Christmas carols. Would you like to hear my favorite, 'Silent Night'?" I always avoided singing songs like "I'll Be Home for Christmas" to patients who could not go home. "Silent Night" created a soft emotional impact.

He listened as intently as I had ever seen a patient listen. When I finished the song, his eyes narrowed and he said, "Do you happen to know the song 'I'll Be Loving You Always'?"

If he had been a physician writing his own prescription, there could not have been a better one than this song. The impact of the words was strikingly real: "I'll be loving you . . . not for just an hour, not for just a day, not for just a year, but always." It was a song of commitment that reflected not just this man's need but the need of all of us to be loved and cared for. As I sang the promise, I became a bit uncomfortable. *What if he expects me to love him?* I thought.

"I failed this time, but I won't fail next time," he muttered when I finished the song. The words fell like stones in the silence.

"What do you mean, Paul?" I asked. I had caught a glimpse of his nameplate above the bed.

"I failed to take my life," he said simply. "Like I said, the next time I try, I won't fail."

My heart jumped, and I was speechless for a

long moment. I had surmounted all the other hurdles—first the needs of long- and short-term-care patients, then the dying patients. But Paul was the first person I had met who had been admitted for attempted suicide. What could I say to him? Intuition told me it would be more important to listen than to talk. I asked only a simple question to open the door: "Why do you want to die?"

He promptly answered my question with a question: "Why should I want to live? I haven't received a card, letter, or phone call from anyone for almost twenty-two months. If I should die tomorrow, no one would cry. I'm not sure anyone would even show up for the funeral."

"Don't you have a family?" I asked, horrified that anyone could be so alone in the world.

"My only son . . . " He hesitated a moment. "My only son was killed in Vietnam. I haven't been able to locate my daughter-in-law and my four grandchildren. The oldest would be seventeen or eighteen by now. I've written to them, but I always receive the same response: 'Moved. Left no forwarding address.' So many times I've wondered what they're doing, and if they're all right."

Paul's eyes suddenly lit up. "You know, life wasn't always this way. There was a time when I was loved. Sometimes those days get very fuzzy in my mind, but music brings the memories back."

Suddenly I remembered the words of a resident I had met in a nursing home in Alabama: "Music—we

"Why should I want to live? I haven't received a card, letter, or phone call from anyone for almost twenty-two months. If I should die tomorrow, no one would cry. I'm not sure anyone would even show up for the funeral."

love it for what it helps us to remember and for what it makes us forget."

"There's a song my dad and I used to sing when we attended a little country church in the Midwest," Paul continued. "Do you happen to know 'How Great Thou Art'?" He stuttered slightly and crushed the remainder of his cigarette in a nearby ashtray.

I strummed the guitar, softly at first, and began to sing. "O Lord, my God, when I in awesome wonder . . . " The chorus was stronger: "Then sings my soul, my Savior God, to thee . . . " A warm, mellow voice joined mine. Paul was singing with me. All traces of stuttering had disappeared. His voice was clear and true. Many patients with speech impairments who cannot remember how to speak in a sentence can sing their favorite songs all the way through. The remarkable thing about Paul was the almost professional quality of his voice.

"You have a beautiful voice, Paul!" I exclaimed when we finished, feeling as if I had just discovered a buried treasure. "Are you a musician?"

"Of course I'm a musician," he said emphatically. "When I was not much more than a kid, I was playing solo trumpet, and I joined a band. I could do anything—hit C above high C without hardly touching the mouthpiece. I could really get up there—bust light-bulbs from the vibrations. Sometimes I played that trumpet till it was white-hot and still heating."

"If you played as well as you sing, that must have been some playing," I commented.

"Aw," he continued modestly, "I sound like an old crow. But I do have a good whiskey tenor." He chuckled to himself. Then he looked at my guitar. "I've been around a lot of hospitals, but I've never seen a guitar in one before. I kind of like the idea."

"Since you're a musician, how long has it been since you've sung or played your trumpet?" I asked.

"I gave up playing long ago," he said. "I haven't really sung for about twenty years."

"Twenty years?" I asked, incredulous. "I can't go five minutes without singing. How did you pull off an absence of twenty years?"

"Well, to tell you the truth, I haven't felt like singing. I've been alone for twenty-six years. In fact, the music brings back a lot of memories. Both my father and my mother loved music. It sort of brings back the good about the past and reminds me of a time when life was worth living. I wasn't always alone, you know. I had a beautiful family. But that was a long time ago."

He lit another cigarette. "I should get rid of these things," he said, looking disdainfully at the cigarette. "They're terrible for your health. The doctor says they're bad for my circulation. Living a long life doesn't mean that much to me, so I guess I've never tried to stop smoking. It's the same with alcohol. After high school I started driving a cab. It was then that I was introduced to alcohol.

"Things went from bad to worse, and I lost one job after another. After I got married I was having so many drinking problems that my wife was going to leave me. Well, I talked her into giving me another chance. We drove out to California to a town just this side of Los Angeles to look at a business that the two of us could run. On the way back there was an accident. My wife was killed. I don't know why I was saved. I used to pray every night that I wouldn't wake up in the morning, because I was so lonesome. I still pray that . . . "

It was Christmas Day, a day when most people were praying for safety, protection, and abundant life. Paul was praying for death. I had heard that the suicide rate soared during the holidays because the celebration of families accentuated the pain of those who were alone. But Paul was not a statistic yet, and I prayed he would not become one.

"Well, I really started hitting the bottle after that," he continued. "My son was staying with relatives by then, and for about a week I drank steadily. I never ate a meal. I drank anything that came along. I wasn't fussy, so long as I could get drunk and stay drunk. That's when I made my first suicide attempt. I took a box of sleeping tablets. Two or three days later I woke up in a hospital. I had had a long sleep, but I was still alive.

"About that time a cousin of mine helped me to get a job at a state mental hospital. I'd been in the medical corps in the army and was the son of a doctor, so I guess it came natural for me. Then I had a stroke.

It was Christmas Day, a day when most people were praying for safety, protection, and abundant life. Paul was praying for death. But Paul was not a statistic yet, and I prayed he would not become one.

Arthritis and circulation problems also began to set in, and I haven't been able to work since then.

"I moved into an old boardinghouse on the west side of town here in Bloomington, and on the twenty-first of December I decided again to end it with tranquilizers and alcohol. I woke up in this room the next morning, clear-headed but a failure at suicide again. I can't do anything right."

Suddenly a wonderful thought hit me. "Sounds like you did okay when you were working in a hospital," I said casually. "Ever thought of volunteer work?"

"Not really," he said. "I've never done anything like that before."

"Every Thursday we have a sing-along downstairs in the activity therapy department," I said carefully. "We sure could use a voice like yours. Why don't you try it for half a day?" I almost chuckled. I knew what half a day could lead to.

"Do you really need me?" he asked.

"Of course we need you," I retorted. "Why do you think I asked?"

"I still sound like an old crow," he said, "but I guess I'll try it." He tried to sound reluctant, but his words were shining with hope.

The afternoon sun had gone down and it was getting dark. I knew there would be no time to sing for other patients. But that was all right. I had come to the right room.

"Since you haven't had a letter for almost two

years," I told him, "I'm going home to write you a long letter, and I'll even bring it to you in person. In the meantime, our volunteer supervisor will come by to talk to you."

I picked up my guitar and turned to leave. I had just reached the door when I heard Paul's voice from the stillness: "Jesus sent you here today, didn't he, for my Christmas present."

"Yes, Paul, I believe he did."

The activity therapy room in the long-term care unit looked different when I walked into it the first Thursday after New Year's Day. The walls had the same colorful posters, and handmade gifts and pillows decorated the shelves. The same residents were sitting around the table, busily occupied. The big difference was Paul, sitting in the midst of them, grinning from ear to ear. I took off my coat, rubbed my hands to warm them up, and sat down beside him. He was almost bursting with things to tell me.

"Ever since you came into my room Christmas Day and got me to singing, things have been starting to click!" he exclaimed. "The volunteer supervisor came into my room last week and introduced herself. She talked to me for about thirty minutes and told me that as soon as I got out of the hospital, she would put me to work. So when the doctor came by on rounds, I said, 'Doc, get me out of this hospital!' He looked at me like I was nuts. He said, 'Why?' I said, 'Volunteer service

I picked up my guitar and turned to leave. I had just reached the door when I heard Paul's voice from the stillness: "Jesus sent you here today, didn't he, for my Christmas present."

wants me to go to work.' He said, 'How about today at noon? Would that be soon enough?'"

"That's fantastic, Paul!" I responded. "What are you doing in your new work as a volunteer?"

"Well, I help get residents down from the floors for activities, and I help take them back to their rooms after therapy. I don't take all of them—just my share— and I help get the wheelchairs down again for dinner. I'm tired. It hurts me to walk sometimes, but I don't feel much pain, because I feel like I'm helping somebody else. I used to feel so doggone sorry for myself, remembering what I used to do and what I couldn't do now. It's the thought of 'nothing' that drives people to suicide."

"Looks like you have a lot more to do now than nothing," I observed.

Paul smiled and began to tell me his experiences—how he'd helped a lonely patient named Louie. How he'd helped Harold, who'd become lost on the floor, find his way back to his room. How he'd held the hand of an elderly lady who needed comfort.

Within a year's time Paul contributed seven hundred hours of service to the hospital. He loved all the work he was asked to do, but his favorite day of the week was Thursday, the day of our long-term-care sing-along. After carefully choosing the songs he wanted to sing, he practiced them and then sang out with the confidence of a seasoned performer. He especially loved the old songs: "Let Me Call You Sweetheart," "Down by the

He was hospitalized for some time, and then finally the difficult decision had to be made to amputate his leg. But Paul never once gave up. "There are a lot of things I can do from a wheelchair," he said.

River Side," and our favorite, "Ain't She Sweet." To the latter song, Paul would add such embellishments as, "Ain't she sweet, oh, yeah! / See her comin' down the street, oh, man!" No one could sing it as he did.

Paul had tremendous empathy for those who were lonely and vulnerable. Whenever any of us were unable to come to the hospital because of illness, mysterious cards would appear in our mailboxes, always signed, "Get well soon. We love and miss you. Donald Z. Duck." For a while, no one could figure out just who Donald Z. Duck was.

One day in the activity therapy room, Paul was busy helping a resident paint ceramics. "Have you ever heard of Donald Z. Duck?" I asked.

For a moment Paul registered surprise. His grin was sheepish. "How did you know it was me?"

"I had a feeling it was you," I said, smiling. "Why do you do that? Why do you always remember us with these funny notes and cards when we're not feeling well?"

"I remember what it's like to be forgotten," Paul explained. "You see mail come along in the hospital, and they pass it out but skip you. I just decided that's not going to happen to any of my friends."

"The next time you get sick, Paul, I'm going to send you a dozen cards," I promised.

He looked me straight in the eye and said, "I'd rather have *you*."

There remained the problem of his family. Staff

members, residents, and volunteers in the hospital had become Paul's family, but the missing members were still on my mind. Some of us had a birthday party for him and gave him an elaborately decorated cake inscribed "Happy Birthday, Donald Z. Duck." We had a special Christmas party for him in the unit his first Christmas with us, and invited him into our homes for dinner on occasion. But I knew he yearned to be in touch with his daughter-in-law and four grandchildren.

After many long-distance calls and much searching, I still had not located them. I decided to write to one of the editors of the *National Enquirer* because I had heard they could find anybody anywhere. Not long afterward, I received a letter from Malcolm Balfour, an editor, telling me the family had been located and the editors sincerely hoped Paul would once more enjoy being a part of a family.

I called Paul's family, full of excitement, only to learn that his son had not been killed in Vietnam. He was very much alive. Due to past emotional wounds, still unhealed, he had disowned his father. He told me he did not want to be in contact with Paul—yet he was willing to tell me about the children, about their ages, their talents, and their progress in school.

When I returned to the hospital, I was not sure how much Paul was comfortable with me knowing, so I revealed my information slowly. "Paul, we've finally located your family."

"Maybe my son was not killed after all," Paul said cautiously. "Maybe he was just a prisoner of war."

I knew then that I could tell him everything I'd learned. I also knew it had been easier for him to admit the absence of his son than to admit the absence of his son's love.

When I was finished, he said, "Thank God they're all right. That's all any man would want to know." It was the last time Paul ever talked about his family.

After a year of volunteer service, he suffered a toe injury that failed to heal. He was hospitalized for some time, and then finally the difficult decision had to be made to amputate his leg. But Paul never once gave up. "There are a lot of things I can do from a wheel-chair," he said. "I can still help with the activities, shave the male residents, and sing in our sing-along."

Though his volunteer service was more limited after that, he continued to serve until circulation problems damaged his kidneys. He was readmitted to Mennonite Hospital with kidney failure, to the same room where I had first found him.

Paul did not have to die alone. He was surrounded by people who loved him and appreciated all he had done to make life happier for them and for others.

The last time I saw him, he said, "You know that Christmas Day you came into my room? I'm so glad you came, because I didn't really want to die. I just wanted to learn to live. And I have. I've had two of the

The last time I saw him, he said, "You know that Christmas Day you came into my room? I'm so glad you came, because I didn't really want to die. I just wanted to learn to live."

greatest years of my life. At first I figured you'd run out of my room when I told you why I was in the hospital. Most people think anyone who tries to commit suicide is nuts. But you didn't leave. You stayed and listened and played your guitar. When you walked out that door, every desire I had to drink—or to die—walked out with you. Because you loved and accepted me, I began to love and accept myself. Now I kind of like myself. You taught me to do that."

"No, Paul," I said. "You were the teacher. You taught us so much about living and loving."

He smiled wisely. "I didn't teach you a thing you didn't already know."

In that same bed, in room 381, Paul died a few days later. His wallet contained a faded piece of paper, a poem I had hurriedly written and given to him:

> One day a stranger crossed my way
> Upon the road of life.
> He was tired of the stony path
> And weary of the strife.
> I had no gift of gold
> Or wreath to give that day—
> So I gave his heart a song to sing
> As he went along life's way.
>
> Snow covered all his cherished dreams
> As he walked through life alone.
> He seemed to have no special friends—
> No home to call his own.

"When you walked out that door, every desire I had to drink— or to die— walked out with you. Because you loved and accepted me, I began to love and accept myself. Now I kind of like myself. You taught me to do that."

But God sent him a message clear:
He had a work to do.
Now he works, he gives, he laughs, he lives,
To strengthen me and you.

And even when discouragement
Makes other people sad,
Paul is there to cheer them up
And make their spirits glad.
He never stops to count the cost
Or think about the pain—
And when a friend has fallen down
He picks him up again.

We love you, Paul!

DEANNA EDWARDS *has a deep interest in music therapy, traveling throughout the United States and to other areas of the world to present workshops to those in the health-care industry and at colleges and universities. She is the author of* Music Brings My Heart Back Home, *where this story was first published, and* Grieving: The Pain and the Promise. *A singer, author, and composer, she has recorded eleven albums, many with songs written for people with special needs. She served for three years on the Foundation Board of Directors for the American College of Health Care Administrators and was selected as one of fifty American Heroines by* Ladies Home Journal. *This story was reprinted with permission of Deanna Edwards, Rock Canyon Publishers, 777 East Walnut, Provo, Utah. (©1996.)*

Christmas:
The Grand Visual Aid

Barbara B. Smith

Last year was the Christmas it all came full circle. Douglas, my husband of over fifty years, and I had begun our customary, joyful Christmas Day rounds. We both still held an inner glow from our Christmas Eve spent with our ever-increasing realm of children, grand-children, and great-grandchildren, who had all gathered at our home for dinner, a Christmas Eve program, and one gift that didn't have to wait until morning to be opened—all this tradition had begun with both Doug's and my own grandparents generations earlier.

On our circuitous course, we were fulfilling another generations-old Christmas custom, that of vis-iting the homes of each of our grown children on Christmas morning to see what Santa Claus had brought their little ones. But that has never been the principal reason we go. We really go because, in the midst of the annual excitement and anticipation of unwrapping all those brightly adorned presents under their Christmas trees, each aglow with tinsel, ornaments, and lights, our families pursue varied means to keep the spirituality of Christmas vibrant and joyful. And we rejoice to be part of that.

As we nurtured and raised to adulthood each of the seven infants that blessed our home, we were always aware that "what we desire our children to become, we must endeavor to be before them." (Andrew Combe, *Home Is Where You Hang Your Memories* [Fort Worth: Paul Brownlow Publishing Company, 1993], p. 20.) Throughout the years we also followed the counsel in Deuteronomy regarding the commandments, applying that biblical directive to all gospel truths, to "impress them upon your children. Talk about them when you sit at home and when you walk along the road, when you lie down and when you get up." (See Deut. 6:6–7.)

Especially at Christmastime, when our family circle is most complete, do we best see the fruition of our gospel efforts in the lives of our children. And this was never more true than in this particular year, as we arrived in time to participate in the gift-opening with most of our families, or, as we continued our rounds, as we recalled wonderful events from Christmases past. This synthesis of Christmases past and present crowned a wondrous new realization for me, opening my eyes regarding our lifelong endeavor to teach our children to know, live, and love the gospel and Jesus Christ, that we might have our family together forever.

Our first stop Christmas morning is always at Sherilynn's, our youngest daughter. Last year we enjoyed our involvement there as Sherilynn and Hector's young family first opened their presents, then ate their traditional Christmas breakfast with us as their guests. Finally we all sat in a cozy circle in the front room, bowed our heads in a prayer of gratitude, and took turns reading scriptures and discussing their significance to Christmas. We read of Samuel the Lamanite's prophecy concerning the signs of the Savior's birth and of Nephi's account of Christ's appearances and teachings to the Nephite nation. It was a delightful beginning to another memorable Christmas Day tour.

Our opportune stop at Barton and Louise's allowed us to watch their family also open presents as they read the biblical narrative of Christ's birth and ministry. Barton paused at several junctures in the story to have the children unwrap presents that both related to those specific parts of the scriptural account and were of current interest to them. For example, when reading of the shepherds watching their flocks by night, the youngsters unwrapped wool sweaters. At the point where the wise men brought gifts of gold, frankincense, and myrrh, there were gifts of money and perfume. When reading of Christ asking the fishermen to "Come, follow me," the boys' packages revealed fishing poles, chest waders, and other fishing gear.

At Blaine and Becky's home, each family member had received a carved name plaque that included the meaning of the person's name. The interpretation of each name signified the potential of the individual in the plan of life and exaltation, even as Jesus' name bore specific import and promise by definition: "Jehovah saves," the one to "save his people from their sins" (Matt. 1:21); "Prince of Peace" (Isa. 9:6); and "Redeemer of the world" (D&C 19:1).

Paired with scriptures, the children's names each carried divine promise:

David—*Beloved one* . . . "The beloved of the Lord shall dwell in safety by him; and the Lord shall cover him all the day long" (Deut. 33:12)

Sarah—*Princess* . . . "A chosen generation" (1 Pet. 2:9)

Scott—*Traveler* . . . "Go ye into all the world, and preach the gospel to every creature" (Mark 16:15)

Steven—*Crowned one* . . . "And when the chief Shepherd shall appear, ye shall receive a crown of glory that fadeth not away" (1 Pet. 5:4)

Brian—*One of strength* . . . "The Lord is my rock . . . fortress . . . deliverer; my God, my strength, in whom I will trust" (Psalm 18:2).

Thus were Blaine's children being taught they had the privilege and responsibility to fulfill the promise of their names given at birth as Jesus, our Exemplar,

I heard about the shepherds, the star, the angels, the wise men, and the Holy Baby long before I went to school. Because of that, I never remember a time when I did not know Him.

had honored his own name during his divine earthly mission.

As we continued our journey that day, we remembered a Christmas before when we had arrived at Lillian's home late in the morning. The whole family was radiant with yuletide warmth and love, and I had been moved to tears when I learned why. Annually her family chooses a symbol from the Christmas story; that year it was angels. But Lillian did not know what culmination to their Christmas theme her husband and children had secretly planned for her.

Very early that Christmas morning her husband, Claron, had called up the stairs, awakening Lillian from a short sleep to hurry down to the Christmas tree. There she found her six children, four girls and two boys, all dressed in new white Christmas outfits, waiting for her, gift in hand. Her heart melted at the scene before her. Each child then presented her a gift wrapped in pure white, telling Lillian why she was "my angel mother."

It was a supernal experience. Of that moment, which was forever sealed in time, Lillian expressed, "Now when I look at my children, I remember them that day dressed in white and realize all the more how I want to be with them throughout eternity."

A few Novembers earlier, Catherine, Carl, and their children had moved into a new home. When Christmas Day grew near, as a family they decided to visit every person on the block and make themselves acquainted with their new neighbors. As gifts to bring,

This last year it was as if Christ had entered into our family circle, enveloping each of us in his warmth and love, filling our hearts with peace and gratitude, deepening our joy and understanding of the true meaning of Christmas.

they baked cookies and decorated little baskets to hold the treats. This first pre-Christmas Day tour of the new neighborhood was such a success that the visits became a tradition cherished by the neighbors, who told Catherine's family, "Our Christmas begins with you!"

Through their retelling of this annual enterprise, we were able to discern the developing faith of her family in the ways of Christ, as well as their love for him and their understanding of the blessings inherent in encircling others in the arms of the Savior's love through their own actions and love. There has been no doubt that Catherine and her family know the essence of the Holy Birth.

Lowell's family was another where the pre-Christmas experience set the tone for the actual holy day. One year, without telling their five children first, Lowell and Lynne chose a night close to Christmas for the whole family to sleep under the Christmas tree. The surprised and delighted children, once snuggled in their sleeping bags, gazed into the gleaming lights of the tree. One suggested, "Let's sing Christmas songs." So they sang the wonderful old carols that testified of the miraculous birth, ending with "Silent night! Holy night! All is calm, all is bright . . . " (*Hymns of The Church of Jesus Christ of Latter-day Saints*, 1985, p. 204.)

As the song ended, another Christmas cherub proposed, "Let's play 'I spy with my little eye' some of the things on the Christmas tree." They did until they

could spy no more. Finally, one awestruck little fellow asked, "Is this the real night of Christmas?" That night proved a memory to last a lifetime and the beginning of another family tradition. He and all of them had felt the love and warmth of the reason for the season.

For our final Christmas Day stop last year at our firstborn Sandra's home, her three-year-old grandson, who lives in Nevada, provided bounteous Christmas Spirit as Sandra conversed long distance with him by telephone. Barely more than a toddler, and blessed with splendid voice and features, brown-eyed Erik sang in harmonious tones for "Granma Fish" (he can't quite say "Smith" yet!) of the Baby "A-sleep, a-sleep, a-sleep, a-sleep, a-sleep, the Savior in a stall! A-sleep, a-sleep, a-sleep, a-sleep, a-sleep, the Lord of all." (*Children's Songbook* [Salt Lake City: The Church of Jesus Christ of Latter-day Saints, 1989], p. 42.)

Erik's mother, Julie, who is Sandra's oldest child, also told of Erik's delight with the early Christmas present from Granma Fish. Sandra had given him a finger puppet set of the characters from the manger scene. With his two-week-old sister, Kylie, in Mom's arms, his father would read the Bible story while Erik worked the puppets with great flair. When it came time to do other things, big brother Erik always put the puppet manger scene back, each character in its proper place.

For little Clarry, Ashley, Michael, Katlyn, and Emily, more great-grandchildren of our sixth generation of tradition, at Christmastime or any time, one of those "other things" to do is to be read to as they sit on a parent's lap. Christmastime for them particularly brings stories of Jesus, retold to this youngest generation by their parents with the same excitement they felt when they first heard those tales of the wondrous birth. Now, reading from storybooks new and old, even some tattered but treasured ones, my great-grand ones listen enraptured, eyes all aglow and their beautiful faces wreathed in smiles.

It all takes me back to when I was a small child upon my mother's knee as she told me the stories of Jesus. I heard about the shepherds, the star, the angels, the wise men, and the Holy Baby long before I went to school. Because of that, I never remember a time when I did not know Him. Douglas declares as well concerning his heritage in Christ, "He was taught to me from my first breath and I have always believed in him."

From the first breaths of each of our seven children and throughout their lives, Douglas and I have tried to nurture faith in Christ, his birth, life ministry, atonement, and resurrection. Now we see this faith actualized down to the last generation. Because of this generational faith, our family knows the truth found in the scriptures which announces that children's children are a crown to the aged, and the glory of the children are their parents. (See Prov. 17:6.) In truth, I prefer not to think of myself as "aged," but I suppose one cannot have great-grandchildren and still be considered young! No matter at all. No small portion of my present joy

I felt like the blind man made to see. My eyes had been opened to see that the simplicity and grandeur of the Savior's teachings span all generations.

I could see that Christ, the Master Teacher, utilizes each Christmas to tap every tender feeling, every holy symbolism, every good thing that would draw each of us to him in such a way that he can enfold us in the arms of his everlasting love.

comes from those of my progeny who have chosen innocent and righteous lives.

This last year's experiences, combined with those of the past, are my proof of the effect upon our posterity of our application as parents and grandparents of the Psalmist's words: "We will not hide them from our children; we will tell the next generation the praiseworthy deeds of the Lord, his power, and the wonders he has done." (See Psalm 78:4.) Of course, each of them, child or adult, and all future links to our line, just like all people, must choose for themselves whether to embrace Christ and his gospel or to settle for something less. We are all afforded such diversity within that "strait and narrow path" (1 Ne. 8:20) of living according to the commandments of the Lord. That so many of my family, although not all, have "chosen the good part" (2 Nephi 2:30), I view, as mother and grandmother to them all, to be the eventual fulfillment of the gospel plan in their behalf—"to bring to pass the immortality and eternal life of man" (Moses 1:39). It is therein that we will truly come full circle, not just at Christmastime, but in the gospel as a whole, forever inseparably connected as individuals and families within the exalted circle of eternity.

This last year it was as if Christ had entered into our family circle, enveloping each of us in his warmth and love, filling our hearts with peace and gratitude, deepening our joy and understanding of the true meaning of Christmas. As many of my children and grandchildren ponder about and engage in more significant gospel study and spiritual enterprises than did we, their actions enlarge my hope that the rising generations are grasping the greater vision, embracing Christ in their lives now and eternally. Even as Douglas and I were taught, then taught our seven children with increased insight and capacity, so have our children taught their posterity with skills superior to our own, as are those children exceeding their parents' bounds.

In that realization it all came full circle for me; it made perfect sense to me. I felt like the blind man made to see. My eyes had been opened to see that the simplicity and grandeur of the Savior's teachings span all generations. I could see the effects of his wondrous works and the seal of a personal witness in the lives of those I love most. I could see that Christ, the Master Teacher, utilizes each Christmas to tap every tender feeling, every holy symbolism, every good thing that would draw each of us to him in such a way that he can enfold us in the arms of his everlasting love. With understanding and gratitude I bowed anew in humble adoration before the Master. Through the grand visual aid of Christmas, my eyes had been opened to the enormous privilege of teaching children and of learning from them as we all grow in faith together.

Each of those Christmas experiences of the children are visual, spiritual, intellectual aids by which they are learning of the Master and the master plan. Whether they learn that in the unwrapping of "spiritual" gifts, in

the correlation of scriptures, in grasping their birthright, in serving others, in the singing of carols, or by being enveloped in the warmth of Christlike love, in all these ways and countless more are avenues to bring them to Christ, in mind, heart, and spirit. It is a masterful part of teaching the plan to his children of promise.

And what I see and visualize for our family is available to all, indeed, to all those who "love his appearing." (2 Tim. 4:8.) The essence of the eternal plan is that every person, every home, every generation will choose to bow and live in humble adoration because Jesus the Christ was born. Christmastime helps us do that freely and with joy.

BARBARA B. SMITH *was called in 1974 to be general president of the Relief Society, a position she occupied for nearly ten years. She is the author of several books, including* The Love That Never Faileth, The Light of Christmas, Growth in Grandmothering, *and* A Fruitful Season.

Christmas Eve in Jail

KURT BESTOR

T HE FIRST CHRISTMAS away from home is always tough. But spending Christmas thousands of miles away from home in a communist country gives new meaning to the word *tough*.

My first Christmas as a missionary was spent in the Language Training Mission where, after the rare treat of sleeping in until 7:30 A.M. and a morning full of letter writing and scripture reading, we ate a fantastic Christmas dinner. Later that night all the missionaries watched the holiday movie *Scrooge* and then fell asleep with visions of mysterious Christmas futures dancing in their heads.

Nearly a year later, after nine months of living in Belgrade, Yugoslavia, I had grown accustomed to the difficult language, unique traditions, and quirky government of the land. But, as the Christmas season approached, I suddenly felt like a stranger again. I missed the magical glow of Christmas lights, the sweet smell of holiday cooking, and even the commotion of a crowded shopping mall. Although the Serbian Orthodox Church held Christmas services, they followed the Julian calendar—which meant "Bozic," or Christmas, fell on January 7th—and those who attended church were usually older and certainly few and far between.

The week before Christmas (according to our calendar) was an especially difficult time. No letters had come from home. No zone conferences were planned— if there had been, at least we would have been able to meet with our missionary "family." There were only two Latter-day Saints in the entire city, and they were planning to be with family and friends. Elder Todd Zagorec and I found ourselves very much alone. Then we received a very unique Christmas gift.

In a communist country, where it was illegal to tract door-to-door, receiving the very rare referral was always a thrilling moment. We excitedly opened the letter from the mission home in Vienna, Austria, and began reading.

"*Name of Referral:* Tomislav Stankovic

"*Town:* Guca

"*Country:* Yugoslavia

"*Reason for interest:* After reading the Book of Mormon, I had dream in which Joseph Smith appeared and told me to join the Mormon church. I would like to know where to find his church."

There was no telephone listed, just the town where this gentleman lived. After consulting our map of

Serbia, we found that Guca was a tiny dot outside the slightly larger dot called Cacak. After hurriedly packing a few changes of clothes and some religious pamphlets, we boarded the next train for Cacak. Upon arrival, we boarded a rickety bus for Guca, having no idea who or what we would find there.

As the bus driver announced that we had arrived in Guca, Elder Zagorec and I stepped out of the bus and into a sleepy little village that could have been 1878 just as easily as 1978. We asked a few villagers if they knew Mr. Stankovic and learned that he lived forty-five minutes away, up the mountain. At this point, our "purse and scrip" was depleted, so, just like disciples of old, we headed up the mountain on foot.

We arrived at the Stankovic farmhouse around dusk, exhausted but exhilarated by the fact that we were on the verge of our first baptism. What a perfect Christmas gift! But our expectations were immediately dashed—the little wrinkled man who answered the door informed us that his son, Tomislav, was living in Austria and had been for several years. Our disappointment must have been apparent, because he extended his gnarled hand and invited us in to eat a holiday dinner with him and his wife. The meal was delicious and much needed, but it did nothing to feed our aching spirits.

Then, in typical Yugoslavian fashion, they opened their home and hearts to us, inviting us to spend the night. They insisted that we take their beds while they retired to the small couch and settee in the

Our disappointment must have been apparent, because he extended his gnarled hand and invited us in to eat a holiday dinner with him and his wife. The meal was delicious and much needed, but it did nothing to feed our aching spirits.

cramped living room. We gratefully accepted. It was Christmas Eve, thousands of miles from home, and it was as good a place as any to celebrate the Yuletide.

Shortly after my companion and I had settled down for our long winter's nap, our visions of sugarplums were interrupted by a loud rap on the door, after which two Yugoslavian *Milicija* burst into the room. Startled and confused, we bolted from our beds and nervously watched as these two burly policemen searched our bags. Luckily, most of our religious material was back in our Belgrade apartment. They did, however, look at us quizzically when our Mormon dictionaries and pamphlets were found. I passed up the opportunity to ask if they "wanted to know more" and started to put my clothes on as they had ordered. Using only a few grunts and gestures, they indicated to us that our stay at the "Hotel Stankovic" was over. I'll never forget the look on our host's face as we sheepishly left. I'm sure the topic at the coffee shop the next day was the "U.S. spies caught napping in Serbian village!"

Our forty-five minute walk up the mountain was replaced by an amusement-park-like ride down. Sitting in the backseat of a Zastava (a car designed for two passengers and low gas mileage), Elder Zagorec and I pondered our fate. I remember praying furiously between bone-jarring bumps on this winding mountain thrill-ride.

Finally we arrived in Cacak and were escorted into the police station. After experiencing a hasty search of our belongings by another policeman, we were placed

After experiencing a hasty search of our belongings by another policeman, we were placed in a small holding cell. The sound of the heavy door closing behind him was deafening.

in a small holding cell. The sound of the heavy door closing behind him was deafening. After a long, strained moment, I looked up at my companion and started whistling the theme from *Mission: Impossible*. Somehow it didn't seem funny to him, and I realized that both of us really wanted to hear the sound of Christmas carols instead of the pounding sound of the jail cell door. The idea of the smells of spicy wassail, fragrant pine boughs, and sweet hot chocolate never appealed so much as they did then. It was the loneliest I've ever felt. Would this be our last Christmas in freedom?

Early the next morning—Christmas morning—the police captain entered our cell. It was no wonder that he was in charge—he looked the most imposing of all the policemen we'd encountered. He took one last look at our passports, glanced suspiciously back at us, then threw them back at us and told us that the U.S. Embassy in Belgrade had vouched for us and that we were free to go.

As we stepped out into the crisp air of the Christmas dawn, the Lord's gift of freedom, taken for granted by a young, impressionable missionary named Elder Bestor, had become a precious gift that I still count as his most prized Christmas present.

KURT BESTOR *is an Emmy-Award-winning composer nationally known for his numerous film scores, television themes, symphonic works, and thirteen music CDs, including his bestselling* A Kurt Bestor Christmas.

Home for Christmas

ARDETH GREENE KAPP

SINCE I GREW UP in Alberta, Canada, I never had to dream of a white Christmas. There was always plenty of snow and cold at Christmastime. At least that's how I remember it.

I also remember, besides the cold temperatures, the feeling of warmth, that happy feeling of being together as our parents, four aunts, uncles, and many cousins of all ages gathered at our grandparents' big three-story house, where we remained from Christmas Eve clear through New Year's Day.

This tradition must have seemed strange to the folks in our small town of Glenwood, since all of our aunts and uncles and cousins lived within walking distance of each other all year long, only a few blocks away from each other. It was not inconvenient for our dads and brothers to return home night and morning to milk the cows, do the chores, and be back in time for our large and happy family breakfast and evening supper. During the morning we played games and listened to favorite stories told and retold by our grandmother as we gathered around the large grate in the floor that let the heat pour out from the furnace below. In the afternoon we practiced for the evening's talent show while our mothers made pies and cakes. I don't remember what our dads did during the day, but they joined us as we all gathered for supper; and after the evening meal we presented a talent show to a very responsive audience, who all sang together. We had a family orchestra and it was agreed, especially by our grandpa, that we were a very musical family.

One of the family secrets we kept and seldom discussed except at Christmastime was the unusual accommodations that were available for the older boys in the family. In the attic of Grandpa and Grandma Leavitt's house, the elders quorum had arranged to store the long wooden boxes they had made for coffins; these would be used as the need arose, at which time the Relief Society would finish the inside of the box with padding and with beautiful white satin. Sleeping in the box-like coffins was a ritual our brothers quite enjoyed until one year when Uncle Ted, unbeknown to the boys, took a resting place in one of the boxes in the corner of the upstairs attic. Of course, light sleeping the night before Christmas was to be expected—the slightest sound would awaken you to the possibility that Christmas morning had finally arrived. This particular Christmas night, around midnight, Uncle Ted made a sound, then raised up from his sleeping position covered with a white sheet. Christmas morning came very early that year, at least for the boys in the attic.

Our Christmas morning tradition required everyone to wait at the top of the stairs until we could all go down together and gather around the big Christmas tree in the parlor. We had decorated our tree with strings of popcorn and cranberries. At the bottom of the stairs we waited for what seemed an awfully long time while Grandpa gave the family prayer. I remember wondering if the reason he prayed for so long was that all together we made such a big family. It seemed to me that each year, as our family grew bigger, his prayers got longer.

After the presents were opened and the wrappings were put away, we, as many as possible, climbed on the sleigh with big runners. The horses would pull us through the snow, leaving deep tracks behind us as we made our way to the river where old Brother and Sister Opstal lived. I could never understand their broken English, and when I gave Mrs. Opstal Grandma's raisin pie, I wondered why she cried.

All these things occurred many years ago, but the memory of being together as a family for Christmas burns as brightly in my mind today as the flames in the fireplace that kept us warm.

I have a little pillow that hangs from our fireplace all year long. The message reads, in cross-stitch, "All Hearts Return Home for Christmas." The quiet yearning to be home for Christmas does not diminish after child-

I have a little pillow that hangs from our fireplace all year long. The message reads, in cross-stitch, "All Hearts Return Home for Christmas."

hood or after marriage. Since my husband's parents were not living, it seemed essential that we travel from Utah to Glenwood, Alberta, Canada, every Christmas. It didn't really matter that our car was old and the tires were smooth, that there was no money in our pockets, that the tuna fish sandwiches became very soggy by the second day, and that the radio announced that due to hazardous road conditions people should not travel except in emergencies. There was no question in my mind that being home for Christmas was an emergency.

Over the years we learned that a benevolent and loving Father in Heaven must have appointed angels to be round about us and over us as we traveled the treacherous highways that would take us home. One night, off the road in freezing temperatures and a blizzard that made visibility impossible and life-threatening, we waited long enough to be very cold and realize our total dependency on the Lord. After fervent prayers, in the distance the lights from a big truck approached us. The driver rolled down his window and shouted through the storm, his words revealing his disgust that we were out on a night like that; he even complained about his own foolishness to be on the highway. I'm sure he didn't recognize himself as an angel sent from heaven in answer to our urgent plea for safety, despite what may have been poor judgment on our part. But, poor judgment or no, we had to respond to the urgency we felt about being home for Christmas. Each year, so long as my parents lived in Canada, we went home for Christmas. Finally, eventually, I learned that you can be home for Christmas in Utah even though Christmases aren't always white.

In 1992, after many years of Christmas in Utah, Heber and I returned to Canada, where we would be for the next three years. This time we were not in Alberta but in British Columbia, and we were not with our family but with over four hundred fifty wonderful missionaries over the course of three years, who indeed became our family.

Through that experience we became awakened to a new and wonderful dimension of the idea of being home for Christmas. A mission would bring the first Christmas away from home for most missionaries, maybe all of them. It would be quite a different experience from the traditions of family gatherings they were accustomed to. I wondered: Can a branch of a pine tree, tied inartistically with a bit of red ribbon, and a candle on a table in a humble missionary apartment make a Christmas? Would they hang their stockings, and if they did would they fill their own or each other's? What about the lights on the tree they were used to? What about all the good food? Could they experience a real Christmas away from all the family traditions that seem to make it real?

Our mission covered a very large area, some of it accessible only over snowy and treacherous mountain roads. We couldn't bring the missionaries all together, but we could go to them and meet in small groups. Could this be like Christmas, I wondered? We began our zone conferences early in the month of December.

After the usual training, we gathered together for a Christmas program, hoping to create a spirit that in some way would focus on the true meaning of Christmas without fueling the feeling of homesickness that was already obvious in the countenances of some. The program began with a readers' theater. Each one, taking turns, stood and read a part of the Christmas story, first from the Bible and then from the Book of Mormon. Hymns were sung at appropriate intervals, supporting the message being read. In some zones, soloists added greatly to the quality of the performance.

In each small gathering of young elders and sisters, the zone leader addressed the group, speaking with excitement, enthusiasm, and conviction of the plans for a white Christmas. In the northern end of the province, there was no question they would have a white Christmas. They could have a white Christmas on the First of July (Canada Day) it seemed to me. In Vancouver, it wouldn't be snow but rain for sure. But the zone leader (each in turn) was undeterred, insisting it would indeed be a white Christmas. Then he would clarify: Can you see yourself dressed all in white? he asked. Can you see yourself with the investigator you are teaching, praying for, and loving with all of your heart? Can you see him or her also dressed in white, ready to enter the waters of baptism together? Can you feel the joy of Christmas in the greatest gift ever given? Will you strive to bring that gift of eternal life to a brother or sister this

They didn't talk of turkey and trimmings; they spoke of fasting and prayer. They didn't speak of packages to be unwrapped, but of gifts of the Spirit. They didn't speak of spending but of saving— saving souls.

year by your diligence and obedience, as you teach with the Spirit and testify of what you know to be true?

As each of these young leaders stood before his group and spoke of a white Christmas in his own way, the message was clear. This is the season we commemorate Christ's birth, his mission, his life, his love, and his atonement, one elder explained. "For behold, the field is white, all ready to harvest," and we can have a white Christmas, he insisted. They didn't talk of turkey and trimmings; they spoke of fasting and prayer. They didn't speak of packages to be unwrapped, but of gifts of the Spirit. They didn't speak of spending but of saving—saving souls.

In the beautiful city of Vancouver, about twenty of the foreign-language-speaking missionaries stood on a platform in the center of the large mall and sang songs telling of that holy night. These young men, in white shirts and dark suits, sang to the passersby in their own language, first in Mandarin, then Cantonese, then Vietnamese and Spanish. People stopped, listened, felt something inside, and wondered and lingered. It was easy to step up and simply say, Would you like to know something about these young men, and why they are here, and the gift they have for you? Some agreed to have the missionaries come to their home and bring the "gift": a message of hope, of peace in a troubled world. The message of eternal life, the restoration of the gospel of Jesus Christ for all mankind in every language and every land.

There were many dressed in white who entered

the waters of baptism that Christmas season. It was a white Christmas for sure, with nothing missing. Everything that mattered was there and so much, much more. If we were not home for Christmas, surely we felt closer to our ultimate home than ever before. I began to review in my mind the highlights of my childhood memories of Christmas, and in a magical way it was as though every piece was in place, now magnified by years of experience.

I met a Chinese couple, recent converts, who took me in memory to dear old Brother and Sister Opstal. I couldn't understand their broken English, and I didn't have a pie to give them, but the gift the missionaries gave them of the gospel of Jesus Christ filled their eyes with tears of joy and gratitude. I understood better now why there were tears in Sister Opstal's eyes.

We didn't have musical accompaniment except for the piano—no family orchestra or grandpa to lead the music—but the Spirit was surely present at each zone conference as the missionaries stood and sang the songs of Christmas. They always ended with "Silent night! Holy night! All is calm, all is bright," which seemed to open a conduit between heaven and earth. They didn't sound like the Tabernacle Choir, and they couldn't sing the Hallelujah Chorus, but as I listened, not with my ears but with the Spirit that was present, I wanted to stand and shout "Hallelujah" with an increasing sense of the true meaning of Christmas.

There were few, if any, of the traditional Christmas lights to adorn the humble apartments of

There were many dressed in white who entered the waters of baptism that Christmas season. It was a white Christmas for sure, with nothing missing.

these young missionaries, but the traditional Christmas lights would be paled by the light that shone in the eyes of the missionaries and the newly baptized members as they came forth from the waters of baptism. It was a light penetrating the darkness of the world not just at Christmastime, but all year long.

One Chinese brother, a convert, had lost his wife through cancer just before Christmas. Funerals are hard at any time. I stood and looked at the coffin so beautifully lined with white satin, and the memories of my childhood Christmas played across my mind. Now the thoughts of death brought to mind the message of eternal life and the deeper understanding of the Christmas story. Christ's life, his mission, his death, his resurrection, and how the meaning of the atonement takes away the fear of death, especially at Christmastime. It was explained to the children that their mother had returned home, home to our Heavenly Father. She would be home for Christmas.

The missionaries received boxes of socks and ties and broken cookies, but their list of wants this year could not be purchased with money.

At the close of each day, with our energy spent, we found ourselves on our knees in lengthy prayer as we pleaded for our little band of stripling warriors in the great army for Christ, both as a group and individually. Looking back now, I see that Grandpa's prayers were not so lengthy as I had remembered them being.

The days were marked off on the calendar as Christmas came and passed. We waited anxiously for

The missionaries received boxes of socks and ties and broken cookies, but their list of wants this year could not be purchased with money.

the letters the missionaries wrote each week, reporting on their highs, their lows, their successes, their discouragements, their challenges, and their victories. After many weeks it became quite easy to detect in the first sentence or two the success or struggle that contributed to the "growth experience" that week. Then the letters following Christmas began to arrive, and with few exceptions the same messages were repeated over and over: "My best Christmas so far." "I've never had such a feeling of love as I've had this year." "It never gets better than this." "This was a real Christmas." These young men and women celebrated the birth of Christ as they represented him and testified of him, as they invited others to follow him. They knocked on doors and exclaimed, "We have come with a message from Jesus Christ about his birth. May we come in?" With this simple and sincere approach, they did enter into the homes, the hearts, and the lives of many. They taught of home, our ultimate home, and our family relationship.

Another year came and went. It was one week before Christmas in the second year of our mission. New missionaries were arriving and others were returning home, having completed their missions. Something wonderful and magnificent happens for missionaries between the time they arrive in the mission field and that day (which initially seems so far away) when they return home. Their experience is paralleled in the story of the wise men. Let me explain.

Matthew gives the account of the wise men

going in search of Jesus. They found him and offered him their gifts of gold, frankincense, and myrrh. "And being warned of God in a dream that they should not return to Herod, they departed into their own country another way." (See Matt 2:11–12.) While Matthew says correctly that they took another route to avoid King Herod, there is a more significant message in this account. The wise men, having found the Savior, went home "another way." Having found the Christ Child, they were never the same again; they could not go back to their old ways.

During a mission, during the days and weeks of tracting and teaching and struggling and growing and testifying of Jesus Christ; through the experience of being filled with the power of the message confirmed by the Holy Ghost, even when it seemed stormy outside; through the experience of feeling they were off the highway in a snowbank, with the passersby shouting words of disgust and abuse—through all this, yet the missionaries found Him. It was not as a babe in a manger, as the wise men found, but they found him and we heard them testify, "He is my Lord, my Savior, my Redeemer, my God." They found him and were ready to return home "another way," filled with a witness of the Spirit they could not deny. They came as young men and women, became true disciples of the Lord Jesus Christ through their missionary experiences, and would return home another way.

"Will there ever be another Christmas like this

"Will there ever be another Christmas like this one?" questioned one, bearing testimony of the power of the Spirit he had come to know.

one?" questioned one, bearing testimony of the power of the Spirit he had come to know.

The answer is yes—if we continue to follow the Lord's way. President Howard W. Hunter told us how, with these impelling words: "We must know Christ better than we know him. We must remember him more often than we remember him; we must serve him more valiantly than we serve him." (Conference Report, April 1994, p. 84.)

It is in the mission field that we all come to know him better, remember him more often, and serve him every day, sharing his message not just at Christmastime but all year long. If we will do that, not only as missionaries, but as their "fellow servants," we will find him in our hearts and in our homes and in our lives. If we will bring our gifts—not of gold, frankincense, and myrrh, but of service, sacrifice, love, testimony, and good will—we will find him and go home another way.

The little pillow still hangs on my fireplace with the message, "All hearts return home for Christmas." When our hearts are right we can be home for Christmas every day.

ARDETH GREENE KAPP *recently returned from the Canada Vancouver Mission, where her husband, Heber, presided from 1992 to 1995. Before their mission, Sister Kapp served as general president of the Young Women organization of the Church. A popular author and speaker, she has written several books, including* My Neighbor, My Sister, My Friend; The Joy of the Journey; *and* What Stripling Warriors Learned from Their Mothers.

"I Was in Prison . . . "

Michael Ballam

C HRISTMAS IS A TIME of miracles. Perhaps the greatest of all is the changing of the human heart.

I became aware of that power a few years ago when I heard a very dear man by the name of Thad Carlson, our stake president, tell his experience of visiting the inmates at our local jail at Christmastime. I was so taken by his story that after his speech I went to him and asked if he would allow me to go with him the next time he went. Of course, my request was made in the heat of an exuberant moment—I didn't really expect that he would take me up on it!

The following Christmas morning at 9 o'clock the phone rang. It was President Carlson. "I'll be by to pick you up in a few minutes," he said. "No, actually, I'll meet you down there." I had no idea what he was talking about. It was not until after he had hung up the phone that I realized he was talking about the jail. I told my wife where I was going, stole away from my family as they were opening presents, and went down to spend just a moment at the jail. I am ashamed to admit I had to look in the phone book for the address. It is difficult to do as the Savior said in Matthew 25—"I was in prison, and ye came unto me"— if you don't even know where it is!

I took with me a plate of cookies my children had made. As I arrived at the jail, having never been inside, I tried the front door and found that it was locked. I was actually relieved and was ready to go back home when a voice, somewhere overhead, said, "What are you doing here? Who are you?"

I explained who I was and why I was there, and then the voice said again, "What is that in your hand?"

I said, "It's a plate of cookies."

I heard a conversation going on in the background, and then the voice said again, "You must leave the cookies there."

I said, "Well, they're just from my children. They made them, and wouldn't it be all right if I brought them in?" I heard some more conversation and then was given permission to bring the cookies and myself through the glass doors.

I proceeded to another set of glass doors and found them locked also. I heard the same voice telling me to proceed forward and to go to another set of doors. At this point, as I was hearing each successive set of doors lock behind me, I became aware of the fact that this was serious business. This was not a common kind of Christmas morning visit, and I was wishing that I was not present. Then a door opened, and there stood President Carlson, beaming, with his happy smile and his firm handshake as he greeted me on a merry Christmas morning.

I walked in to see a very small space that had room for six folding chairs, three on each side, with just enough room for one person to pass between the rows. He said, "There are thirteen inmates here today, the thirteen who were not given leave to go during the Christmas holidays, and they are going to be released in just a moment. Those who wish to will come and hear what we have to say." That plural pronoun loomed out to me. I was here to observe, *not* participate!

Within seconds I heard the opening of thirteen cell doors, in unison, and expected to hear twenty-six anxious feet coming to greet us, but there appeared to be no sound coming from the cells. Again I was relieved and ready to return home. Then I became aware of one young man coming down the hall. I was stunned beyond belief as I looked at him. Somehow I expected that all prisoners in our local jail would resemble a grizzled Humphrey Bogart or Edward G. Robinson. Instead I saw a young man with beautiful black hair, institutional attire of "hunter orange" color and slippers, and a countenance I couldn't see because he was looking at the floor. As he approached President Carlson he was met with "Good morning! Merry Christmas!" and a

As I arrived at the jail, having never been inside, I tried the front door and found that it was locked. I was actually relieved and was ready to go back home when a voice, somewhere overhead, said, "What are you doing here? Who are you?"

proffered handshake. The young man refused the hand-shake, looked President Carlson in the eyes and said, "Oh, yeah? Exactly what's good about it? What's merry about this Christmas?"

President Carlson said, "It's a beautiful morning with a skiff of snow on the ground sparkling like dia-monds."

The young inmate replied in an angry tone, "That's great, man. You come here and tell me what it's like out there. Have you noticed I'm in *here?* That's great!"

President Carlson answered in a loving tone. "If you will come over here and look through these win-dows at this angle, you can see the snow." The young man followed the directives to where I was standing there at the window, and I was able to view at close range his expression. It began as a look of wonder and longing at the sight, but quickly changed to one of anger and hostility. At that moment he began a profane tirade about why he was there. It was the fault of the lawyers, the judge, the parole officer. Everyone was to blame for his being there, with one exception: him! But at that particular moment I did not feel compelled to explain that principle to him.

At that point, I was sure *I* didn't want to be there, and I couldn't possibly understand what input of signif-icance I could offer in the situation. Then I saw another inmate walking toward us, looking very much like the first, and then another, making three inmates who had come down to see what was going on. They sat on the folding chairs across from each other and I sat down too, waiting to hear what in the world President Carlson could have to say to these young men on this Christmas morning. The statement he made left me stunned: "Gentlemen, we're pleased to be here this morning, and now Michael Ballam would like to talk to you."

In spite of how much I adore President Carlson, the sixth commandment came to my mind! I had absolutely nothing to say. I hadn't come with a speech, and I certainly didn't know what I could possibly say to these men. As I looked at the inmate across from me, who was so close our knees were touching in uncomfortable proximity, I recognized he was wearing a rosary and a cross. I asked him if he was a Catholic, and he said he was. I told him that I had sung for the pope, which seemed to catch his attention.

"*The* pope?" he asked.

"Yes," I answered.

He asked me why I had sung for the pope, and where it had happened. I told him it was in the Vatican—that I was a soloist with an organization that went to sing one of Schubert's magnificent masses for the pope, and that a most unusual thing had happened.

The pope knew that we had prepared the Schubert Mass, and we knew he knew and loved those pieces of music, but instead he asked us if we knew any Negro spirituals. I answered that of course we did, and we sang some spirituals for him. The boy asked me why

I thought he had wanted to hear the Negro spirituals as opposed to the great work of Schubert that we had prepared. I could only answer by saying that there is something innately powerful about the sound of the black Southern slave. Their lives were circumscribed by bondage and they had only two means of deliverance: one was through Jesus, and one was through death. So they sang about both, Jesus and dying.

As I was explaining this, the thought occurred to me that I knew a song, a Christmas song, in fact, that was typical of a black Southern slave spiritual, and I began to sing:

> Sweet little Jesus boy,
> They made you be born in a manger
> Sweet little holy child,
> Didn't know who you was.

> Didn't know you'd come to save us, Lord,
> To take our sins away,
> Our eyes was blind;
> We couldn't see,
> We didn't know who you was.

> Long time ago you was born,
> Born in a manger low,
> Sweet little Jesus born.
> The world treat you mean, Lord,
> Treat me mean, too.
> But please, sir, forgive us, Lord,
> We didn't know it was you.

As I looked at the inmate across from me, who was so close our knees were touching in uncomfortable proximity, I recognized he was wearing a rosary and a cross. I told him that I had sung for the pope.

Sweet little Jesus born
Born long time ago,
Sweet little holy child,
And we didn't know who you was.

The feeling in the room changed, and the young man who had been looking at the floor was now looking me directly in the eyes. He said, "I wish I weren't here today. I wish I was home with my kid." Tears came to his eyes and he began to talk about why he was there and how he could get out and how he could change things. I'm convinced that all the speeches I could have labored to write could not have touched this man's heart like this simple song about a blessed baby.

Music is miraculous. It is one of God's most eloquent languages. It cuts through politics, race, religion, education, and economics and speaks to the heart. I know that the Spirit of our Father in Heaven dwells in music, particularly in the music associated with the Christmas season. It was there when the Savior was born. It was there when he died. It will be there when he comes again. What a blessing from him to us here below!

MICHAEL BALLAM, *founder and general director of the Utah Festival Opera Company and professor of music at Utah State University, continues an international operatic and recital career and is a sought-after lecturer and clinician. But perhaps his most important performances are given at the bedside of the elderly, disabled, or terminally ill, or in the classroom as he teaches little children of the wonders of Beethoven and Mozart.*

The Worst Christmas Pageant Ever

ANN EDWARDS CANNON

I WAS FOURTEEN and I wanted to die.

Part of the problem was that I was fourteen and female. My brother John, the doctor, says that being fourteen and female is a disorder actually recognized by the American Psychiatric Association, and that his professor once spent a whole day talking about it in his Introduction to Psychiatry class. Physical symptoms of the fourteen-and-female syndrome include slumping in chairs, standing with arms folded across the chest, and wearing the exact same clothes as other disturbed fourteen-year-old girls. Behavioral symptoms include crying, trying on lip gloss, crying, going to the mall, crying, talking to disturbed fourteen-year-old boys on the telephone—and crying.

It's a terrible disease, and so far there's no cure.

So being fourteen was definitely part of my problem. The other part was that I was supposed to be the featured Youth Participant in the ward Christmas program that Sunday. It wouldn't have been so bad if I had just been allowed to get up and deliver the standard Youth Talk, which runs something along these lines: "Today I'm going to talk about (fill in the blank). Webster's Dictionary defines (fill in the blank) as (fill in a couple more blanks). I hope that we can all (blank, blank, blank)." And so forth.

Well, I wasn't going to be allowed to give a Youth Talk. I had to participate with a bunch of adults in a special holiday program written and directed by Dr. LaVerl S. Wanship, professor of music.

Dr. Wanship was a roly-poly little man who could play the piano like nobody's business. In fact, he could play the piano so well that sometimes he would stop in the middle of bearing his testimony and say, "Why don't I just play my testimony for you?" Then he would stride up to the front of the chapel on his little legs, position himself in front of the piano, pause—and play. Whenever Dr. Wanship did this, I and the rest of the fourteen-year-olds in the ward would cringe. It was so *embarrassing*.

Actually, Dr. Wanship wasn't the only adult in our ward who did embarrassing things. There was Sister Miller, who wore white go-go boots even though she was seventy years old, and Brother Meacham, who sprayed spit every time he talked, and Sister Fisher, who loudly told everybody at a ward party that all it took to keep regular was a cup of bran and a glass of warm water every morning.

Even my own parents were embarrassing. Although they were always late to sacrament meeting, they breezed through the door at the front of the chapel and headed straight for the family pew instead of sitting circumspectly in the cultural hall stealing Cheerios from babies with the rest of the stragglers. "You guys never come on time," a friend once whispered to me. "And why does your mother wear those black sunglasses in church, anyway?"

It was true. My mother, after arriving late, proceeded to sit through church meetings looking like Jacqueline Onassis avoiding the press at the airport. It didn't matter that she was the most terrific-looking mother in the whole ward, not to mention the universe—I still wanted to slip like so much loose change through the cracks of a sofa.

And now I was supposed to do something embarrassing, too.

Dr. Wanship called a practice the Saturday before the program so we could rehearse our parts. We met in the chapel and took turns reading our parts from the podium while Dr. Wanship sat on the front pew and flapped directions at us.

"It's your turn, Sister Edwards."

I schlepped over to the microphone like any self-respecting fourteen-year-old girl, plopped open my mostly unused Bible, and began to mumble.

I schlepped over to the microphone like any self-respecting fourteen-year-old girl, plopped open my mostly unused Bible, and began to mumble.

"I am the light of the—"

Dr. Wanship leaped like a toad. "NO! NO! NO! Listen to the words you're saying." He placed his hands over his heart. *"Feel* the words you are saying."

I stared at Dr. Wanship. Putting too much Dippity-Do in my bangs was something to get worked up about. Reading scriptures wasn't.

"Try again."

I did. He flew at me again. And again and again.

"He wants me to make a total fool of myself," I wailed to my father that night.

My father looked like Job would have looked if the Lord had sent him a fourteen-year-old daughter along with the rest of the plagues. "Just do the best you can," he said patiently.

So the next afternoon I stood before the congregation, tossed my hair, and routinely read the words,

"I am the light of the world: he that followeth me shall not walk in darkness, but shall have the light of life." (John 8:12.)

When I sat down, I saw a look of profound disappointment cloud Dr. Wanship's round little face.

Well, Dr. Wanship, that was more than twenty years ago, and it has taken me that long to understand why those words once made the night glad. So I want to apologize for letting you down and to tell you that I would try to read those words for you now the way you hoped I would then. I would make those glorious words

I stared at Dr. Wanship. Putting too much Dippity-Do in my bangs was something to get worked up about. Reading scriptures wasn't.

ring from the chapel walls. I would make them crack stone.

Merry Christmas, Dr. Wanship.

ANN EDWARDS CANNON *is a freelance writer whose publications include* The Shadow Brothers; Amazing Gracie; I Know What You Do When I Go to School; *and* Cal Cameron by Day, Spiderman by Night. Great Granny Rose and the Family Christmas Tree *will be released by Deseret Book in the fall of 1996. This story was first published in* This People, *Winter/Holiday issue, 1989.*